DOCTRINE AND WORD
Theology in the Pulpit

MARK ELLINGSEN

John Knox Press
ATLANTA

Library of Congress Cataloging in Publication Data

Ellingsen, Mark, 1949-
Doctrine and Word.

Includes bibliographical references and index.
1. Theology, Doctrinal. 2. Sermons, American.
3. Lutheran Church—Doctrinal and controversial.
4. Lutheran Church—Sermons. 5. Preaching. I. Title.
BT78.E44 1983 230'.4133 82-21311
ISBN 0-8042-0533-7

10 9 8 7 6 5 4 3 2 1
Printed in the United States of America
John Knox Press
Atlanta, Georgia 30365

To
Betsey

Contents

Introduction

Those of us who think of ourselves as theologians are quite concerned about the minimal impact of theology on the contemporary church. In recent decades the ministry of many congregations in virtually every denomination has been carried on without a sense of the relevance of theology. Instead, the guiding paradigms for ministry have either been therapeutic or managerial. Of course these are valid tools for informing ministry, but if they become the church's guiding principles the uniqueness and power of its proclamation seem undercut. In this regard, the discontent of many Christians in mainline denominations over what they perceive to be a secularization of the church may in fact have some theological validity.

The problem is not a lack of dedication or faithfulness among church leaders. Rather, because we have become unsure about the significance of traditional theological doctrines for daily life, theology has been displaced from its role of guiding the church's ministry. Psychological and management techniques seem far better suited to play this role because their practical relevance is more readily apparent than that of theology. To reverse these trends the theological community must begin to articulate the significance of traditional Christian doctrines for daily life with more power and force. The relevance to life of this book is an attempt to contribute to that work.

The format of the book reflects this concern for relevance. With the exception of the first, each chapter deals with a specific doctrine from two distinct, though related, perspectives. The first section of each chapter provides a description of the doctrine, its biblical and historical roots, and a theological analysis of the way in which the doctrine has been dealt with by various Christian traditions. I have sought to be ecumenical in my presentation, noting the different ways Christian communities treat the doctrine. However, because I believe this theological variety is legitimately grounded in Scripture I have sought to describe the virtues and deficiencies of each alternative.[1]

Having provided this biblical and theological background for each doctrine, the second section of each chapter turns to the question of its significance for daily life. This is explored in a sermon on a biblical text, which reflects on and has its meaning informed by the doctrine considered in the chapter. I would not dare suppose that these portions of the book provide any definitive statement of the significance of the doctrines. Unlike the first portion of each chapter which endeavors to provide some definitive analysis of the doctrines, the sermons represent my own reflections on how these doctrines have interpreted my life, and how they have illuminated my relationships with others. In so doing the sermons also demonstrate that Christian theological reflection is relevant to the issues of daily life. Persons cannot exist without interpreting their lives in relation to some categories which make sense of their experience. The sermons illustrate how Christian doctrines can be viable tools for making sense out of our everyday experience and also that they need not function merely as Sunday morning rhetoric but should be living, relevant concepts. I hope that the sermons will encourage others to exercise their own creativity in reflecting on their lives in light of the doctrines and the biblical accounts they summarize. If I have succeeded in this regard or at least helped readers to reconsider theology's relevance for their ministry, this book has fulfilled its aim.

A book like this, which is in effect one man's summary of the Christian faith, will inevitably contain deficiencies. It can in no way pretend to provide a completely adequate treatment of its subject, and as I glance over the Contents page, I am only too aware of its shortcomings. For example, there is no chapter devoted exclusively either to ministry or to social ethics, although both issues are dealt with in the context of other doctrines. My only excuse for my summary treatment of these topics is the nature of this volume. It is conceived as a popular presentation of Christian theology. Such a book demands conciseness and the linking together of related topics which would otherwise deserve separate attention. Thus I hope readers will draw no conclusions about the relative importance I place on certain theological issues from the way I have organized this book. Nor, hopefully, will my easy summaries and typologies be regarded as failure to appreciate the complexity of theological problems. That is work for another day; my task here is to simplify the complex.

In regards to the book's organization I am also uneasy about my decision to treat the doctrine of God and the doctrine of the Trinity in separate chapters and about the conclusions some readers might draw from my consideration of sin prior to Christology. About the latter issue let me say that I have simply followed the logical-narrative order of salvation. The problem (sin) precedes its remedy (Christ). Yet from this it should not be concluded that I believe we must first clarify and define the human predicament before the gospel makes sense. On the contrary I would follow the Reformers' view that sin is only properly known in light of the gospel.[2] In regards to the separate treatment of God and the Trinity, I hasten to add that the Christian doctrine of God will not be properly treated until the third chapter on the Trinity, for God is known truly only in three persons. The chapter on God is merely a discussion of the formal concept of God with attention to the apologetic question of what sense it makes to believe in God at all in our contemporary world.

As a final comment in regard to the book's structure, it should also be noted that I have not considered doctrines related to how we know about the Christian faith—doctrines of revelation, Scripture, and tradition. I felt I could not and should not deal with these complex issues in a volume such as this. The position one takes on these issues reflects one's theological method. Thus I was faced with the choice either of expounding my own views or trying to schematize the various other methodological approaches. Such a topic deserves a book in itself, not a few chapters of exposition. In light of these considerations and because I thought questions of method did not properly belong in this kind of practical introduction, I have elected to omit these issues. I do not think the book's failure to consider them damages its usefulness since the doctrines of revelation, Scripture, and the like should be formal considerations. Thus one can present the material content of the Christian faith with clarity and integrity without reference to these issues.

It might be well at this point to say a brief word about my methodological suppositions so that readers will not think I am unaware of them. In fact I am currently working on another project which delineates my suppositions more fully in relation to other homiletical-exegetical approaches. The ecumenical presentation of both the doctrines and the sermons in this volume reflects a kind of literary-narrative (canonical) approach to theology. By a literary-narrative approach I have in mind the kind of theological proposals made by Hans Frei and George Lindbeck, and related approaches of their Yale colleagues like Paul Holmer.[3] I am much in debt to them and to all my teachers; however, they are in no way responsible for errors associated with my own particular use of their insights.

Basically I find myself intrigued by the efforts of narrative theologians to redefine the theological task as it has been understood since the enlightenment. While most theology since the eighteenth century has sought to interpret Scripture and Christian doctrine in light of our contemporary experience, the narrative approach reverses this process. Our contemporary experience is interpreted in light of the biblical accounts and Christian doctrine. We are to appreciate the storylike character of Scripture, and like any good story Scripture will wrap us up in its tale. It becomes life-orienting when we identify ourselves and our world with its characters and events. For example, Peter's denial (Mark 14:66–72) is only properly understood when we realize that the story is also about how, though we deny Christ all too often, he forgives us and goes to meet us in Galilee (Mark 16:7). In the same fashion our contemporary situation is only rightly understood in light of the doctrine of sin. This mode of theology will be particularly evident in many of my sermons.

Other implications follow from this narrative approach. It enables Christians to deal with the challenges to Scripture's credibility posed by historical criticism. When viewed as a piece of literature, Scripture's integrity cannot rightly be called into question by historical research any more than *Macbeth's* integrity and meaning are called into question if there were no historical Macbeth. Additionally this attention to Scripture's literary character encourages appreciation of the whole of Scripture and so nurtures a truly ecumenical perspective. As one cannot rightly understand a novel if one skips certain chapters, so Scripture cannot be understood when certain of its portions are overlooked. To embrace Scripture in its entirety, however, entails coming to terms with its incredible variety. Thus a narrative theologian is inevitably led to an appreciation of how legitimate the theological variety in the Christian church is. Precisely how the variety, the ecumenical perspective, that I note and celebrate in this volume can be integrated into a systematic whole is a project I hope to undertake some other day.

As I reflect on my presuppositions and how I have been influenced in my theological understandings, I realize that more should be said about those to whom I am indebted. Even a casual reading of this text will indicate how much my understanding has been shaped by my extended family (both by blood and through marriage) and my friends. Two of them deserve special mention. Our son Pat was intimately involved in the creation of this book. His occasional visits to his father's study helped lend a touch of realism and pleasure to the writing of this book and reminded me to keep things as simple and concrete as possible. My wife Betsey's contribution was no less important. She has been my editor, typist, critic, conversation partner, and best friend. Indeed her contribution to this book has been so profound that she deserves far more than mere mention on the dedication page. For in truth, although this book bears my name on the cover, like everything else I have done in the recent past, it is really our work.

This work begins with an examination of theology's relevance for life today. Before considering the various doctrines we will turn in the first chapter to a discussion of what Christian faith and its doctrines offer contemporary human existence.

Chapter One
THE CHRISTIAN OUTLOOK

What is Christianity? Why would one want to be a Christian? The answer to the first question entails gaining clarity about fundamental Christian doctrines. Once achieved, this provides an answer to the second question about the gospel's relevance. As much as any time in history it is important that Christians understand their faith: theology is indispensable for all Christians. *Theology* is thought about God, specifically, reflection on Scripture and doctrines. These *doctrines* are the principles or rules which, because they are correct expositions of Scripture, govern the Christian community. The theological task, that of gaining a proper understanding of the biblically-based doctrines, must be a high priority for Christians in our contemporary situation. These doctrines help us get our bearings, to know who we are. This is particularly important now in a society that is losing its way.

There is marked upheaval in our contemporary world. Social analysts speak of narcissism, future shock, and the therapeutic mentality in describing Western society. When these dynamics are studied in relation to a proper understanding of the Chrsitian faith, we can begin to discern why one would want to be a Christian. What the good news of Jesus offers people today is identity. By identity I refer to the core of a person which orients everything he or she does. Identity is what makes persons uniquely who they are.[1] The gospel provides this for human beings; it gives one a true sense of who one is.

A sense of identity is an important antidote to the dangers of our present situation. Anxiety about oneself and the future is recognized by analysts as the root cause of the unhealthy societal dynamics we have noted. This anxiety is itself rooted in the gradual deterioration of the societal structures to which we are accustomed. We all have a sense of this deterioration. The old institutions of our twentieth century, liberal, industrial society are not working. Our welfare systems, our political systems, even our economic systems are not working. These old institutions are not functioning efficiently because they are not able to deal with new rapidly changing circumstances. For example, since nonrenewable energy supplies have become less accessible, Western economies have begun to falter. Also refinements in mass communication and trends in the customization of products are challenging patterns of conformity in our society. The rise of special interest political groups is a logical outcome of these trends. As a result of these new realities our political systems, which are predicated on a high degree of conformity and consensus, are paralyzed.

The recognition of the inability of our institutions to cope with these new realities has led to a widespread loss of confidence in them. As a result people are not internalizing the norms and values of Western society as easily as they once did. We can see this in the breakdown of the work ethic, the nuclear family, and the sense of loyalty to one's employer and nation.

When a society's norms do not shape its citizens' outlook on life, the society begins to fall apart. And if a new societal structure is not constructed in the old one's stead, people have no frame of reference for their lives. They become anxious about themselves and the future because they are empty of all meaning and purpose. In our present situation many have sought new ways of defining their lives through excessive preoccupation with the self (narcissism) or through therapeutic means. Since our old points of orientation are losing credibility, ours has become a society in search of its identity. The Christian outlook has much to offer our contemporary situation by providing an answer to this search. Christians are people who have an identity; we know who we are.

It is important at this point to appreciate the interconnections between societal norms and personality/identity formation. A person's attitudes, values, and self-images are not innate in human nature. Rather these features of our identity are the sum total of all the things we have experienced in life. This is why the deterioration of our society's cultural norms is so anxiety-producing for people. When the structures which have shaped our identity are no longer viable we literally lose our own identity. At least we lose those things which lend support to our lives.

Christian faith, by contrast, offers a radically different and more secure foundation (θεμέλιος) for one's identity (Luke 6:46–49; Matt. 7:24–27). The Word of God and the sacraments function as the norms of the Christian community. As such, members of the church have their true, new identity shaped by those norms. In fact baptism and/or faith in Christ gives Christians a whole new identity (2 Cor. 5:17; Rom. 6). This is not to say that Christians' identities are not shaped by other factors (families, education, etc.). Yet it does mean that all these other factors are not definitive for the Christian. ("Whatever gain I had I counted as loss for the sake of Christ" Phil. 3:7.) The Christian's real home, true self, and sense of purpose is given in Christ.

What is the nature of Christian identity? What purpose in life do Christians have as a result of their faith? The remainder of this volume will deal with these questions by articulating the meaning and relevance for life of the fundamental doctrines of the Christian faith. The exposition on each doctrine has been accompanied by a sermon in order to lend insight to the doctrine's relevance. For the present, we have already established the need for theological efforts to understand and interpret these doctrines. Because a sense of identity is what Christians have to offer the contemporary world, we need to be very clear about the content of this identity. One of the functions of doctrines is to describe Christian identity, that is, what Christians believe. Doctrines do this insofar as they provide accurate summaries of the Word of God, which gives Christians their identity. In fact, the reason for the formulation of most doctrines was to preserve Christian identity. Most were formulated at times when it was being threatened by certain heretical movements, and so it became essential to describe more precisely what Christianity is.

Theological reflection on Christian doctrines, then, is not merely an academic exercise. All Christians need to come to an understanding of these doctrines and their relevance in order to understand who they are as people of faith and what they and the gospel have to offer the world. Therefore, theology is a task which is the responsibility of every Christian.

Although we will need to consider all the fundamental Christian doctrines before gaining a more complete understanding of the Christian outlook, by way of introduction, we should provide some initial insights about the new identity Christians have been given and precisely what this identity has to offer the contemporary situation. The sermon which follows will give a viewpoint on this question and outline my theological perspective on how the doctrines function in Christian life. An important consideration in understanding the treatment of Christian identity which I will offer is Paul's and Martin Luther's idea of the union of the Christian with Christ (the Christian as the bride of Christ [Gal. 3:27; Rom. 6:5]). This image conveys the fact that by the grace of God, Christ and believers have entered in so intimate a relationship that everything they have is held in common. Thus all that we have (anxiety, guilt, sin) is given to Christ to bear on our behalf, and all that he has (life, resurrection, love) has been given to us.[2]

This image allows the church to affirm the Pauline doctrine of justification by grace through faith (Rom. 3:24, 28): the idea that all that we have is a gift of God. When we begin to consider what belongs to Christ and what is given the Christian in union with him, then the image of union with Christ provides important insights about a Christian's identity.

One of the fundamental tenets of the New Testament witness is Christ's role in creation (John 1; Col. 1:16–17; Heb. 1:2; cf. Prov. 8:27–30). As Christ is the agent of God's creating the world out of nothing, so his redeeming work on behalf of humanity, the new creation, is an instance of God's ongoing creativity. He is by nature a Creator who is never done with his creating (Ps. 104). Thus to be united with Christ through faith, to share all that he has, is to share in his creative projects. Christians have been made people who participate in Christ's creative work in the world. The Christian's identity is that of Creator who works with God in creating greater good. The following sermon adds a bit more concrete detail to these reflections on the Christian outlook and its significance for human existence.

§

Text: Galatians 3:26–29
(*Preached at a pastors' conference.*)

Analysts of societal trends have observed that we are living in a time of social chaos. Our society is characterized by narcissistic tendencies. Values are up for grabs; there seems to be no stability. People are not satisfied. We do not know who we are. These are not easy times to be Christians, what with everyone being a taker when Christians are called to be givers. But these are exciting times. As much as any other period in the history of humanity the Christian church has a Word that speaks directly to what is happening in society. We Christians have the answer to the question everyone is asking. Paul tells us the answer in various places when he speaks of the Christian's union with Christ. We know who we are. Paul tells us most clearly who we are in Galatians 3:27. "For as many of you as were baptized into Christ have put on Christ" (Gal. 3:27; cf. Rom. 6:5).

Our text tells us that Christians are people who have been united with Christ. In our baptism we have been so intimately connected to Christ that everything which belongs to each of us is shared in common, and so Christ takes on all that we have. He bears our death, sin, and guilt for us. In fact on the cross he has taken them away. We, in turn, have been given all that he has. Christ brings life, salvation, and fellowship with other members of his body. All these are ours now. They make up our new identity. We fall out of harmony with ourselves when we fail to make use of these gifts (cf. Rom. 7:20; Rom. 6:2).

This union with Christ entails at least one additional dimension, one which speaks very directly to the question of who Christians are. We must remember that to "put on Christ" means to share all that he has and is. The New Testament witness is quite clear about one dimension of Christ's person that is too often overlooked. He is Creator (John 1:1–3). And creation is not a once-and-done event. It is ongoing (Ps. 104). God, and so Christ, is always creating, always working for good (Rom. 8:28). Therefore, to share all that Christ has means that we participate in the divine project of creating new good in our world. This is the Christian's new identity. It is what Paul seems to mean when he says we are a new creation (2 Cor. 5:17) and, as such, are free from sin and may now put ourselves in the service of righteousness (Rom. 6:19). Our baptism has made us people who in all things work for good and work together with other members of Christ's body. Whether we like it or not we are stuck with this task and with each other (cf. 1 Cor. 12:12ff.).

To this point I have simply been talking about baptism or faith in Christ in light of what union with Christ entails for us. Have you ever thought about the baptismal life as what makes you who you are? We know who we are, my Christian friends. Our baptism (faith in Christ) has made us people who in all things work with God to bring about more good. In a society filled with anxiety and uncertainty about identity Christians have something: we know who we are.

This whole question of personal identity is an intriguing topic. By identity I mean the "core" of a person toward which everything he or she does is oriented. It makes a person unique. The real me, Mark Ellingsen, is not some mysterious essence hidden under my surface activities. Rather, I am the sum total of all the things I have done and all the things that have happened to me. There is no way I can totally get away from this. I will always be a kid from Brooklyn, with a Scandinavian background and a zest for preaching and theologizing. Although I may not exhibit those aspects of my personality all the time, there is really no way I can have true peace with myself unless I somehow come to terms with those elements. So it is with our baptism (faith in Christ). In our baptism God has made us people who put on Christ, die to sin, and so work to bring about new good in the world. We cannot find peace with ourselves unless we come home to who we are. People in all spectrums of our culture are seeking to find themselves, but to Christians it is given to know who they are.

The Christian church has an exciting Word to speak in today's society. We may live in a post-Christian era. Yet nonetheless it is the case that many Westerners have known the name of Jesus and have been baptized. It is no wonder there is anguish and searching. These people are not in touch with themselves. We have the Word to speak to them: child of God, come home! Jesus died for you; you are a person who dies to self for the sake of the neighbor. This is the real you.

This suggestion seems to offer us a number of things. It says something about how we may regard ourselves as people of faith. It also says something about what to make of one of the major sources of disagreement among Christians. That is the old question of whether you can talk about living the Christian life and still avoid legalism (compromising the centrality of grace). The arguments run hot and heavy.

On one side we find the radical freedom-from-the-law people. I refer to Christians who would not dare whisper a word about a distinct Christian lifestyle for fear of lapsing into legalism. Then there is the opposite viewpoint: those who are afraid that justification by faith might be heard as "Do your own thing."

I have learned much from my friends who emphasize these viewpoints. Yet in the final analysis I think they are extreme views which capture only part of the reality. I do not believe that a Christian need compromise justification by faith when talking about the character of the Christian life as long as it is very clear, *very clear,* that all talk about Christian life is nothing more than a description of our God-given identity, not an order to live a certain way.

For example it would be peculiar for someone to tell me I should start being a better Scandinavian, enjoy theologizing, and love my wife. It seems peculiar to be told I must do these things. They just seem to happen; they are part of who I am. So it is when we proclaim the baptismal lifestyle—the dying to sin for the sake of Christ and the new good of God's creation. This is not something we accomplish; it just seems to happen because of how God has made us. This in no way compromises God's grace because to tell me who I am as a child of God is to tell me what God has done for me.

Of course there are times in life when I lose my way, when I forget who I am. At those times it helps to be reminded about the loves in my life, my talents, my gifts. Sometimes I need to learn again who I am. This is the Word we have for a society that has lost its way: come home, child of God; we know who you are.

Christian friends: Christ has made us creative people, working for good in all things. That is the real you. Now go and do your thing. It is one of God's good gifts to Christians in this time and place that we know who we are. Amen.

Chapter Two
GOD

This chapter represents both the heart of this book, as well as a major transition in its development. The chapter is a transition insofar as we will move from considering the relevance of Christian faith for contemporary life to an examination of specific Christian doctrines. In making that transition we need to consider the question of the intelligibility of the Christian faith. Is it at all warranted to believe in God, given what we know about science, astronomy, archaeology, and the like? In order to deal with this question it is first necessary to consider the Christian understanding of God. This brings us to the very heart of the Christian faith: the doctrine of God. For although Christians focus their faith on Jesus Christ, their faith is in the God who is revealed in Jesus Christ.

Of course the most basic commitment in the Christian understanding of God is *monotheism*. This is the belief that there is only one Supreme Being (God) in the universe. The early Hebrews were among the first of primitive peoples to adopt this viewpoint. In contrast to the common belief of their time in many gods (polytheism), the Hebrews were rigorously insistent that Yahweh, whom they worshiped, was one God, the sole object of worship. "Hear, O Israel: The LORD our God is one LORD; and you shall love the LORD your God with all your heart, and with all your soul, and with all your might" (Deut. 6:4–5).

Of course this early credal confession pertaining to their single object of worship did not in itself constitute the early Hebrews as monotheists. They lived in a polytheistic environment in which their God needed to be recognized as one of many gods, though superior to all (cf. Gen. 31:53; Judg. 11:24; 1 Sam. 26:19). Gradually, however, with the rise of the prophetic movements in face of foreign domination, Israel began to develop a theoretical monotheism. Sixth and even eighth century B.C. prophets came to speak of Yahweh as Creator and God of all peoples (Isa. 45:12; Amos 9:5–8) in addition to whom there is no other God (Isa. 43:10.ff; 45:21).[1] The development of this uncompromising monotheism is an important dimension of the Christian heritage derived from Judaism.

This brings us to the question of what is entailed by having a God: what is the Christian God like? The biblical witness describes God with accolades. There is no being who exceeds God in any way. "I am the first and I am the last" (Isa. 44:6). God is eternal, infinite, and self-sustaining, dependent on nothing for existence (Gen. 21:33; Deut. 33:27; Ps. 93:2). God is holy, exalted over all creation (Ps. 99:2, 9; Isa. 6:3). God is almighty and all powerful (Rev. 4:8; Exod. 6:3). "In his hand are the depths of the earth; the heights of the mountains are his also. The sea is his, for he made it; for his hands formed the dry land" (Ps. 95:4–5). God is the point of orientation for all creation and holds it together; everything is dependent upon God. All life is found in God, "the Alpha and the Omega, the beginning and the end" (Rev. 21:6).

Yet this God, who so far exceeds the most magnificent characteristics of the creation, shares something in common with the creatures. He is personal in nature, capable of entering into relationship and conversation with human persons. This personal character is reflected throughout Scripture by the way in which God addresses people and the personal way they respond to God. Such a personal character in God negates any tendency Christians might have towards *pantheism*, the identification of God with the universe. Christians cannot be pantheists because their God transcends the universe and holds it together. Pantheism is further ruled by God's ability to enter into personal relationships with humans, a characteristic which would be impossible were God identical with an impersonal universe.

In the New Testament certain characteristics of God's personal nature (characteristics which are already implied in the Old Testament) are made clear. In Jesus Christ we learn that God relates to people as a kind and gentle parent; God is "Abba," which means father (Mark 14:36; Rom. 8:15). In short the Judeo-Christian God is a God of love (1 John 4:8; John 3:16). Christian faith basks in the comfort of knowing that the Creator and sustainer of life, the one who so far exceeds all that we are or can be, "is our refuge and strength, a very present help in trouble. Therefore we will not fear though the earth should change . . ." (Ps. 46:1–2). God is our point of orientation, who gives life meaning and protects it. Before such a being one can only respond as the psalmist did: "O come, let us worship and bow down, let us kneel before the LORD, our Maker!" (Ps. 95:6).

The biblical images we have noted provide us with only a partial picture of the Christian doctrine of God and what it means to believe in this God. In regard to the former question, we need to examine the development of the doctrine of God, particularly in the early church. The early church emerged in an intellectual climate which was heavily dominated by hellenistic philosophy. Thus it is not surprising that in developing the doctrine of God the church came to be influenced by Greek ideas, particularly those of Plato.

The point of correlation between Plato's philosophy and biblical insight was the biblical affirmation of God's sovereign freedom. The biblical witness, as we have seen, is quite clear in asserting that God is not dependent on creatures as we are on God. The parallels between this insight and Plato's ruminations on the origin of the world in his treatise *Timaeus* were too inviting to overlook. The Christian concept of God has been unmistakably altered ever since this process of correlation was initiated for virtually all subsequent theological reflection about God has been heavily influenced by Greek presuppositions.[2]

Plato had taught that the origin of the world was the work of a divine artist or demiurge, who took matter and gave it form by imitating the idea of the good. This implied a differentiation between the idea of the good and the Creator. Such a move was unthinkable for both Christians and Jews. However, the platonic understanding was so ingrained in the culture that it became necessary to dialogue with it. The result was that Jews and Christians came to combine both the demiurge and the idea of the good in their doctrine of God. As a result God came to be regarded as possessing the qualities of both the demiurge and the idea of the good. The creative activity of the demiurge seemed to correlate with the biblical witness about God's work in creation. And the idea of the good (which for Plato was incomprehensible, impassable, and infinite) was correlated with God's sovereign freedom. The end result was an impassive, unchanging God, who seems unaffected by human suffering and despair.

To analyze the impact this view of God has had on formal theology since the Patristic period would provide significant learnings about the history of theology. This is a task beyond the scope of this work. For the present it is sufficient to note that the sense of God's distance, the feeling that God is too far removed from our daily lives, which many contemporary Christians experience is directly accounted for by the presence of strains of Greek philosophy in our doctrine of God.

The appropriation of Greek insights by the church tended to overturn the basic Hebrew teaching concerning God's intimate involvement and identification with people. Yet the Hebrew insight is by no means silenced by these doctrinal developments. The very name of the Hebrew God, Yahweh (יהוה), implies a different framework for understanding the biblical images pertaining to God which we have already noted.

The name Yahweh literally translates "He who is," "I am who I am," or "I will be who I will be" (Exod. 3:14). The emphasis on being/becoming in the name Yahweh provides a fundamental insight into the Hebrew view of God. It means that for the Hebrews, God was not a static essence. Rather God was manifested in action.[3] Far from indicating God's aseity, the name of the Hebrew God indicates that God's being is relative, determined by interactions with people.[4]

The consequences of an appreciation of the Hebrew rather than Greek framework for understanding the doctrine of God are profound. It means that the characteristics which we previously observed that Scripture attributed to God must be understood in terms of God's activity. Thus God is holy because God acts in a holy manner; omnipresence is manifest in presence with people. Quite significantly in relation to the doctrine of justification, God's righteousness must not refer to some static essence in God. Rather God must be righteous because God functions to make us righteous. (Note the full development of this insight in chapter eight.)

The impact of this hebraic view for the doctrine of God is that God can be regarded as more involved and more relevant to the human situation. God's very being can be understood through God's interaction with us. Most recently this treatment of the doctrine has been developed by process theologians.[5] Yet their insights are not new. Several other protestant theologians have applied hebraic notions of God's contingency and agency.[6] An ongoing tension between efforts at understanding God and God's attributes in terms of static Greek presuppostions or in terms of action-oriented Hebrew presuppositions is one of the characteristic marks of Christian theology.

The preceding analysis has not provided us with a full picture of the Christian doctrine of God. It has only provided a formal description of God, not captured God's distinct nature. That can only be done once the doctrines of the Trinity and of God's relationship to Jesus Christ have been considered. For God is only known in three persons and through Jesus Christ. Thus this chapter is offered only as a framework in which to understand all succeeding doctrines considered. It in no way properly describes God or the doctrine of God. That task will be more fully completed if the preceding is read in light of the next chapter.

Thus far we have only dealt with our first question, "What is the Christian understanding of God?" We now need to consider the significance of belief in God, as well as the credibility of such a belief given the scientific-secular culture in which we live. Since these two issues are related I shall consider both with initial attention given to the latter.

The problem for Christians is how to find a place for God in a world which no longer seems to need supernatural causes. Since the Enlightenment it has become increasingly accepted by many that the world can get along quite nicely without God. In fact the church has always faced this challenge. In response, some theologians have sought to go beyond a mere appeal to faith as a means of establishing the credibility of belief in God. Rather some have constructed so-called "proofs" for the existence of God.

The first of these proofs was called the *ontological argument*. It was first devised by Anselm, an eleventh-century monk. The argument is based on the internal logic of the concept of God. God, it is argued, is "that which nothing greater can be conceived." If, however, God did not exist then there would be something greater than God since existence is better than nonexistence. Yet nothing can be greater than God. Therefore God must exist.[7]

The second proof of God's existence developed by Christians has been called the *cosmological argument*. Thomas Aquinas, thirteenth-century theologian of the Roman Catholic Church, is probably its prime representative. The argument begins with the recognition of the contingency of events in the world. There must be an ultimate ground of certainty to this contingency. As such the ultimate ground must be a necessary being: God. Thus God necessarily exists.[8]

Other arguments which have been developed for God's existence include the *teleological argument* and the *moral argument*. Both assume a structure similar to that of the cosmological argument. Thus it is argued that order (or design) and morality in the world demand the existence of a divine designer and some transcendent ground for moral values. This divine designer and transcendent ground is God.

Philosophical analyses have called the validity of these "proofs" into question. The possibility of infinite causality damages most of them. Additionally all seem vulnerable to the extent that they are substantiated by appeals to faith and to the Christian tradition's understanding of God. In short the proofs do not seem to be proofs at all, but only extrapolations about the implications of faith in the secular world.[9]

This failure of the proofs leads us to reconsider the question of the credibility of belief in God in a somewhat modified way. I believe that there is something about common human experience when examined from the perspective of faith, which makes faith in God an intellectually credible risk. The very nature of human life demands that we choose some points of orientation for life which provide us with our identity. The following sermon makes that clear, showing that the choices we make provide us with our identity. (In that sense it further develops points made in the preceding chapter.) We have seen in this chapter that the significance of choosing faith in God is that one's identity is based, not on that which is finite and capable of decay, but on God who is Creator, the first and the last, exceeding all we could ever wish and hope for, loving and comforting us. The sermon does not provide a proof for the existence of God or a complete picture of the identity provided by faith or of God's identity. Rather the sermon provides a formal framework in which to understand God more fully through the doctrine of the Trinity, for God is only known in three persons. The sermon also provides a basis by which to understand the significance and credibility of other doctrines subsequently considered. They help provide further dimensions of the Christian's identity.

§

Text: Proverbs 9:1–10

(Preached in a small, blue-collar congregation.)

The fear of the Lord is the beginning of wisdom,
and the knowledge of the Holy One is insight.

This is a lovely image. But how can twentieth-century people accept it as true, as an accurate statement of reality? After all, we know that wisdom does not necessarily begin with God. That is obvious. One need only read one of the latest academic journals to realize that many of our greatest intellectuals are avowed atheists. Such persons have no fear of the Lord, yet who would deny their wisdom? This is a hard question: what do wisdom and the fear of the Lord have to do with one another?

It seems to me that the first step in trying to understand how wisdom and the fear of God relate to each other must be to examine the nature of our text. Earlier when I read the text I said that this lesson is taken from the book of Proverbs, a collection of Wisdom literature compiled by ancient Israel (between the eighth and fifth centuries B.C.). Also recall that for the Hebrews wisdom was not merely academic knowledge; it was not limited to formal education. Rather wisdom was regarded as practical knowledge, the kind of common sense people need to live their daily lives. In other words, since wisdom has to do with how we live everyday, we can only conclude that all of us require wisdom. This means that what the passage from Proverbs has to say is relevant to each one of us everyday.

What is this piece of common sense knowledge which the Scripture has for us? "The fear of the LORD is the beginning of wisdom" (Prov. 9:10). That still does not seem to make any sense. After all, a belief in God does not necessarily follow from common sense. If it did, then the fear of God would not require faith at all; one could prove God's existence just by virtue of acquiring common sense. The trouble is that everybody seems to have a certain degree of common sense, but not everybody knows God, and so what can we conclude? Is it possible that this passage is simply outmoded, something that was once true but no longer applies? Is it possible that while in an ancient culture where everyone believed in God, one might claim that the fear of the Lord was the beginning of wisdom, in today's culture such a statement simply is not true? Perhaps. Yet before we give up on this proverb so easily, let us struggle with it just a bit more.

Maybe one of the problems we have had to this point is that we have spoken in generalities. We have been talking about wisdom or common sense in general, rather than any specifics of which you can grab hold, and so I would like to have each of you join me in an experiment. Think of a certain body of knowledge with which you are well acquainted.

The body of knowledge I have chosen is geometry. In geometry the whole system of knowledge is based on certain basic truths called postulates. For instance, the statements that a square has four sides and that a line is straight are examples of postulates. From these postulates it should be possible to prove everything else. Yet no one tries to prove the postulates themselves. One simply must accept the fact that a line is straight and that a square has four sides. If you do not you never get off the ground. I wonder just how different geometry is from the body of knowledge you chose. Are there not certain basic assumptions or rules that you just have to accept before you can get started? For example, you cannot know anything about baseball strategy unless you first accept its rules. You cannot know anything about driving safely if you do not first accept the basic mechanics of how to operate a car. In fact, you cannot even live your life unless you first accept certain basic premises which provide you with orientation. This is what the eleventh-century theologian Anselm meant when he said: "In order to understand, I must first believe."[10]

What does all this have to do with our Scripture lesson and the doctrine of God? Quite a bit I think. What I am suggesting here is that the credibility of belief in God might be more apparent if we substituted the words "acceptance of basic assumptions" for the words "fear of the LORD." In other words, we might just as well say "the acceptance of basic assumptions is the beginning of wisdom" as "the fear of the LORD is the beginning of wisdom."

What do you think? Have I corrupted the meaning of the passage by arguing that persons' basic assumptions, particularly basic assumptions about life, are really their god? Before you answer that question, listen to the words of Martin Luther:

> A god is that to which we look for all good and in which we find refuge in every time of need. To have a god is nothing else than to trust and believe him with our whole heart. As I have often said, the trust and faith of the heart make both God and an idol. . . . That to which your heart clings and entrusts itself is, I say, really your god.[11]

If we accept Luther's explanation on this point, then there is a sense in which we must say that human beings are religious animals. Since all people have certain basic principles by which they live their lives, every person has a god. Belief in God is not such an absurd undertaking after all. All people have gods who rule their lives; we all begin with some initial leap of faith. The question is what kind of god do we have?

How about you? What is your god? Not so fast with your answer; think about it. Is it not true that far too often the things that we really live our lives for are money, or prestige, or security, or even, praise-worthy though it may be, for family or humanity in general? Is it not often true that from Monday through Saturday these are our gods and that Christianity is something we have relegated to a corner of our lives? What is your god when you are on the job, at home, or in school? Is it always the loving and forgiving God of the Christian tradition? If you live your life at all like I do, I fear the answer to that question is "No." Far too often God is not our god, and we bow down and worship an idol.

I think I hear someone say, "But, Mark, that is only human!" Yes, that is true. Yet someone else might say, "It is sinful to live your life for something other than the Christian God." And that is also true. Of course, that is not surprising since to be human is to be sinful. Yet in the midst of all this, the gospel speaks another word coming softly from the cross. "It's all right; I love you; you're forgiven." That voice can always be heard; it is always calling us, reminding us that we are forgiven people. What else is that but a life of wisdom? It calls us to the "new life" in Christ. It comes with letting God be our God.

What is the most important concern in your life? What gives your life meaning? What is your God? Is it an idol like worldly success or self-fulfilment? The gods people keep are reflected in their lives. Do you reflect finite and decaying things like these or the eternal and loving God who hung on the cross and rose from the dead? The Christian doctrine of God provides us with a new manner of life. Through our faith in this God we are given an identity grounded in fundamental values which will not pass away. Regarded in this light, faith in God seems to make very good sense. To a confused and searching world we Christians can boldly witness that the fear of the Lord is indeed the beginning of wisdom. Amen.

Chapter Three

THE TRINITY

Scripture speaks of a threefold revelation of God. God is known as Father, Son, and Holy Spirit. This is a fundamental tenet of Christian faith. The early church was immediately faced with the question of what to make of this threefoldness of God. Its commitment to Jewish monotheism (see Deut. 6:4) made worship in the name of the Son and the Spirit a problem. Yet devotion to the Son and the Spirit was built into the worship patterns of Christian faith from an early date. (Note that baptism in the name of Father, Son, and Holy Spirit is prescribed in Matt. 28:19.) It should be recognized, then, that the doctrine of the Trinity is not formally outlined in Scripture. Yet the early church's exegesis and practice seems to indicate that this doctrine is a legitimate extrapolation of the biblical witness.

The first formal step in the development of the doctrine is usually identified as the Council of Nicea (A.D. 325). The Nicene Creed, which the church affirms today, is a product of this ecumenical council. The purpose of the council was to affirm that in Jesus Christ a genuine Incarnation has taken place. The formula which was agreed upon essentially affirmed his divinity. Christ was said to be *homoousios* (of the same substance as) with the Father. In asserting this the church rejected two heterodox movements which emerged in the early centuries. It repudiated *Arianism*, the idea that Christ was a creature, unlike the nature and substance of the Father.

It also rejected *Sabellianism*, which regarded Christ as merely a mode of God. Father, Son, and Spirit were regarded merely as temporary modes or manifestations of God. They fulfill their mission and return to the monad. The issues at stake in rejecting these movements and affirming Christ's divinity will be considered more fully in the sixth chapter on Christology.

The Trinity doctrine, as the church has come to accept it, emerged as a result of misunderstandings about the Nicene formula. The idea that Christ was of the same substance as the Father (*homoousios*) unwittingly contributed to the renewal of Sabellianism. In response to this tendency to negate the distinctions between Father, Son, and Spirit and in order to assert the divinity of the Holy Spirit, several defenders of Nicene orthodoxy proposed a formula. The idea of three *hypostases* and one *ousia* was developed, and it subsequently achieved widespread recognition. In the Latin-speaking Western church the term *persona* was substituted for the Greek *hypostases*. Thus we are accustomed to speaking of Father, Son, and Holy Spirit as three persons.

No formal definition of these terms has ever been ratified by the church. The ambiguity which surrounds them accounts for the confusion many Christians have about the Trinity. A variety of the interpretations of the doctrine have been offered. None perfectly grasps the mystery.

It is historically quite clear why the church formulated this doctrine. Like most doctrines it was occasioned by the emergence of heterodox movements which challenged existing practices and piety in the church. In that sense the Trinitarian formulation delimits the outer bounds of Christian faith.

The affirmation of the deity and of the unity of the three persons is also significant, insofar as it functions as an interpretive tool which helps protect Scripture's authority. Without a doctrine like the Trinity, which allows for the distinction of persons, it would be hard to deal with the New Testament's apparent subordination of the Son to the Father (Matt. 26:39; 27:46; Mark 15:34). Also the unity and purpose of the persons is absolutely essential for guaranteeing Scripture's normative character. The intimate unity of the divine persons provides that all subsequent revelation by God through the

Holy Spirit must be in accord with God's revelation in Christ through Scripture. An undue emphasis on new revelation which might contradict Scripture is thereby precluded. The Trinity implies that all new revelation must always be judged by the biblical witness. Additionally, insofar as it implies that the work of all the persons comprises a unity, the Trinity also entails that Christ's redeeming work is not rightly proclaimed apart from attention to the Father's work in creation. The question still remains, though, as to what significance this doctrine might have for our lives today. The following sermon offers some suggestions about what to make of a God who is three *hypostases* and one *ousia* and what significance this has for our relationship with him.

§

Text: Matthew 28:18–20
(*Preached in rural congregation.*)

Today is Trinity Sunday, the day when the church marks the beginning of the second half of the church year. I would like to suggest that it would be good for us to consider the mystery of the Trinity, the triune God.

Now the Trinity doctrine has been for centuries a source of tremendous confusion and embarrassment in the Christian church. If you really level with yourself, I'll bet it has been a real problem for you and your faith. I know it has been for me. In fact, as far back as I can remember, whenever I thought about the Trinity, the triune God, the only mental picture I could get of it was that of a three-headed monster. But a three-headed monster was not a God that I could love; in fact, it was not much of a God at all, but just what it seemed, a monster. As a result, whenever I thought about God or prayed, the last thing I ever did was to think of God as three persons in one. I wanted no part of that kind of a God. So, the Trinity doctrine became something with absolutely no meaning for me. something that became kind of embarrassing since I could not accept it as a part of my faith. I'll bet the majority of you have had some of the same problems I had. With respect to the Trinity we all seem to be in the same boat.

What does this tell us? I think it says that we in the church have not faced up to a most crucial problem. Of course, all of us would agree with Romans 11:33 that God's ways are inscrutable and that God in essence remains a mystery to us. Indeed faith itself is a mystery, but let's face it: to claim that a certain aspect of Christianity is mysterious is no excuse for not attempting to explain it. Indeed unless we have some grasp of a certain doctrine, like the Trinity, we cannot even begin to understand in what sense such truths of faith are mysteries. It seems to me at least, that in order really to appreciate the mystery of the Trinity we first have to make some attempts of our own to understand that mystery.

Initially, it is important to realize that the doctrine of the Trinity, as it stands, is not to be found in the Bible. Of course, Scripture does talk about God as Father, Son, and Holy Spirit, but it never really clarifies the exact relationship between the three. It took many hundred years of debate in the early church to decide what Scripture was saying about this relationship. But finally in A.D. 325, at a little town in Asia Minor called Nicea at a conference in which every religious leader of the church at that time was present, it was decided once and for all that Jesus, as Son of God, and the Holy Spirit shared equally the divine prerogatives with the Father. This concept was more fully developed by later theologians of the same century until finally the whole church came to understand the nature of God as a mysterious union of three persons, Father, Son, and Holy Spirit, as one.

Now I think it is very important at this point to understand that the idea of the Trinity is a doctrine formulated by humans on the basis of what they believed God was like. In other words, it does not exhaust the mystery of God. On the contrary, all the Trinity doctrine does is to try to describe the way in which God is revealed to us. (It does this with the supposition that how God is revealed says something about the essential identity of God.) About that problem I believe the Trinity doctrine has something very simple, yet very important, to say to us. Basically, whenever we confess our faith in a Triune God, we are really saying that we believe God is revealed as Father. In this role God is the Creator of our world and us, the giver of the law and the Ten Commandments, and the righteous judge who both punishes the wicked and rewards the good. Next, God is revealed as Son. In this role God came to us as the man Jesus of Nazareth, our Savior, who died and rose to forgive our sins and to tell us of God's love for all people. Finally, God is revealed as Holy Spirit. In this third role God comes among us, bringing us to faith and being the responsible party for all good on earth. In short, while God is one, God is also revealed in these three distinct forms.

On the surface, of course, all of this sounds strange—but not that strange. After all, don't we also reveal ourselves to each other in different ways? For instance, as I stand before you today I reveal myself as a pastor and preacher. Yet when I am with my wife, I reveal myself to her as husband and lover. And finally, when I'm with my parents I continue to reveal myself as their loving son. So I am pastor, husband, and son—three different "people," as it were, and yet I'm not three, but one. All three people are Mark Ellingsen.

O course, I am no different in this way than any of you. All of us are really many different persons rolled into one. We are child, parent, laborer, homemaker, businessperson, or student. We're all these things and more, and yet each of us is really only one person. Now if all of us can be many different persons rolled into one, can we expect God, who is the most true and genuine person, to be any different? So the doctrine of the Trinity is, above all, a reminder to us that God was, is, and can be known in these three different ways. He is at the very core of his being Creator, savior, and comforter.

Of course, it is not really quite that simple. We human beings are not exactly like God. At this point we come upon the essence of the divine mystery as revealed in the Trinity. We begin to see just how great and powerful our God is, and how weak and fragile we are. For although each and every one of us is many different persons—parent, child, husband or wife—all rolled into one, only God is able to distinguish God from God in the three different persons. In other words, only God can see God as three distinct persons, each independent of the other. Only God can come into a relationship with God; only God can be a friend to God. Think about it for a minute. While I may be at any one time a pastor, a husband, or a son (and maybe all three at once), I can at no time have a relationship or a friendship between myself as minister and myself as child of my parents. I am not really three distinct people; as a minister I am still, at the same time, the child of my parents. I cannot be just one or the other. It is not like I could step outside of myself and be something else than what I am. But God can! Somehow in his majesty and power God can be himself as Father, and yet a totally different person as Son. But at the same time, while being different from himself as Father from the way he was Son. God is both Father and Son. In short, as Father God enters into a friendship with the Son in a way very similar to the way in which I can become a friend to one of you. Yet God is in some mysterious way able to be both people at the same time.

So the Trinity doctrine tells us two things about God. It reveals to us that we are in some way like God because we reveal ourselves to each other as different persons all rolled up into one. And yet, at the same time, the Trinity reveals to us just how different God is from us. While God is three different persons rolled into one, each person is distinct from the other in such a way that we really have three different people like me, and you, and you. This part of the Trinity doctrine is so much of a mystery that words fail to do it justice, and we can only cry out along with the father of the sick child who Jesus healed, "I believe; help my unbelief!" (Mark 9:24).

What does the Trinity doctrine tell us about God? Surely it tells us that God reveals himself to us in three ways, as Father, Son, and Holy Spirit. But it also tells us about the way we as individuals have to relate to God. On the one hand, we have learned that you cannot fall back on pat answers; if you do not try to make some sense out of these mysteries, they will not mean a thing to you. On the other hand, we have seen that if you do not admit to the mystery of God's existence and God's dealings with humanity, then you are left with a God who resembles an old gentleman with a gray beard sitting atop the clouds. A God like that is not worth having anymore than a God who is so mysterious we cannot understand him at all. The two have to be kept together—the God who is so much of a person that in many ways we are just like God, and the God who is so different from us that we cannot begin to know God. If you give up one, you lose the other. Hold them together, and you have a God worth dedicating your life to, a God worth loving, because God loved you first. The message of Trinity Sunday is that such a God exists, a mysterious ineffable God who is at the same time so near that God even knows the number of hairs on your head. Amen.

Chapter Four
CREATION AND ELECTION

"In the beginning God created the heavens and the earth. The earth was without form and void . . . " (Gen. 1:1; cf. Gen. 2:4b). "Then God said, 'Let us make man in our image, after our likeness; and let them have dominion . . .' " (Gen. 1:26). "And God saw everything that he had made, and behold, it was very good" (Gen. 1:31; cf. 1 Tim. 4:4). "But in these last days he has spoken to us by a Son . . . through whom also he created the world" (Heb. 1:2; cf. John 1:3; Col. 1:16–17; Prov. 8:27–30). These four biblical verses encapsulate the essential ingredients of the Christian doctrine of creation: (1) that God is the Creator of the world, (2) it is created out of nothing, (3) the world is not eternal, (4) Christ is involved in the work of creation, (5) humanity is created in the image of God, and (6) the creation is intrinsically good. These essential ingredients have gained ecumenical acceptance in the church, but only after several controversies in the first centuries.

Like most classic Christian doctrines, the doctrine of creation was forged principally as a result of the early church's apologetic stance toward both Judaism and Greek classical thought and as a result of internal disputes with heretical viewpoints. From their Jewish heritage the earliest Christians were led to affirm that God had created the world. This needed to be affirmed over against classical philosophical thought which dominated the Graeco-Roman world of the early centuries. Because this culture was heavily influenced by the Greek philosopher Plato, it was commonly held that God (the Good) and matter were coeternal. Also as we previously noted, the Good was deemed impassable, so transcendent that no direct relationship between it and the world was possible. Thus to the degree that God was identified with the Good, creation of the world by God was not readily accepted in the first century. It was more common to believe that the world had come into existence through the work of some intermediate beings who gave preexistent matter its form.[1]

Given this cultural context, it is little wonder that the Christian understanding of creation was not readily accepted among the intelligentsia of the Graeco-Roman world. The early church found it necessary to distinguish its viewpoint from mainline philosophical currents. Thus, it became absolutely essential for the earliest Christians to assert God's active involvement in bringing the cosmos into being. This cultural situation also led some of the church's theologians to develop the notion of *creatio ex nihilo* (creation out of nothing). The popular idea of the coeternity of God and matter was thereby repudiated. Although this view that God has created the world from nothing has never been formally ratified by any council of the church, it has gained ecumenical acceptance largely because it was embraced by eminent Church Fathers like Clement, Bishop of Alexandria, and Tertullian.[2] It was brought to further prominence in subsequent debate with *Arianism*, the fourth-century heresy, which taught that Christ was a creature.[3]

The framework for refuting the Arians had already been laid by the church's dialogue with classical thought, but not all dimensions of classical philosophy and Judaism were rejected by the early Christians. In fact they found it helpful at points to concede that Christianity did not have a monopoly on the truth and that certain fundamental Christian insights were already inherent in Greek and Hebrew thought. The Stoic idea of the *logos* found ready acceptance in early Christian thought as a means of accounting for the sharing of Christian truths with antiquity.

The Stoic philosophers of the early centuries believed that the universe is subject to a universal reason or *logos*. The logos was understood as the rational structure imprinted into the very fabric of all things. Stoics believed that we could understand reality only because our rational capacities were part of this universal logos.[4] (In short, I can understand what I understand because the thing I have understood is already tied to my very being.)

This concept of the logos lent itself naturally to early Christian thought. John 1 had drawn upon the concept by identifying Jesus with the logos (Word). This made it possible for the early church to argue that the revelation of the logos in Jesus was a completion or fulfilment of what classical philosophy had discovered through reason about truth and reality.[5] Insofar as these philosophies had understood truth and reality they could only have done so through the logos. Thus it must follow that classical thought had some partial awareness of Christ.

Adoption of the logos concept, insofar as it implied that creation had a certain rational structure, facilitated the church's ability to dialogue not only with classical thought but also with Judaism. With this concept the early Christians could speak of a natural law built into the structures of creation. This allowed Christianity to embrace those dimensions of the Old Testament law which were in harmony with the natural law. Again it was possible to say that Christian truth was not radically new but was already implicit in antiquity. Additionally, the church was provided with a critical principle with which to justify its failure to comply with the entire law of Moses. Christians were only bound to those portions of the Mosiac law which were in accord with the natural law.[6]

The logos concept and its connection with John 1 served the church in yet one other profound way. The Johannine notion of the logos' role in creation helped in the development of Christological doctrine in the face of Arian heresy. It is reflected in the Nicene Creed's affirmation of the divinity of Jesus which we noted in the preceding chapter. The creed does not just assert that Christ is *homoousios* (of the same substance) with the Father. It also asserts that through him (Christ) all things were made. In this way Arianism was refuted on several fronts.

As we previously noted, insofar as Christ shares the Father's substance he cannot be deemed a mere creature. Further, insofar as Christ is the principle of creation he cannot be deemed a creature since he had no beginning. In this way we can see how the church's insistence on Christ's role in creation served to undergird its Trinitarian and Christological commitments. By the same token the notion of *creatio ex nihilo* serves these commitments. The agent of salvation who redeems humanity from annihilation can only be he who first brought humanity into being out of nothingness.[7] Only if this agent created the world out of nothing can we be sure of his power to save humanity from annihilation. As such God, not a creature, must be Creator and Savior since by definition a creature could not create out of nothing. God's own being would then be presupposed in the creation. Thus since Christ is savior and only the Creator can save and since Christ is also Creator, creating out of nothing as only God can create, it must follow that if redemption is God's work then Christ must be God. It is in this way that the affirmation of creation out of nothing served to refute the Arian heresy. The tight logical interconnections of this argument indicate how closely the doctrine of creation is tied to the development of other doctrines like the Trinity and the two natures of Christ. In fact on the basis of this analysis it is fair to say that the church's credal formulations are not just concerned with the Trinity and Christ's person. To affirm these is also to imply something about Christian belief in creation and its relation to Christ's redeeming work. (To say Christ is divine is to say that he must be agent of both creation and redemption.)

Our analysis has now shown how the early church's dialogue with both non-Christian and heretical movements facilitated its affirmation of God's creation of the world, creation out of nothingness, the idea of a natural law in creation, and Christ's role in creation. An unambiguous affirmation of creation's goodness also emerged as a result of controversies in this early period, specifically as a refutation of the second century heretic, Marcion, and a later heresy, *gnosticism*.

Marcion was apparently heavily engaged in the early church's efforts to distinguish its teachings from Judaism. In his efforts to assert the newness of the gospel, Marcion went too far. For him the gospel obscured all else in the world, in fact negated the world. Marcion could not reconcile evil in the world with the goodness of the gospel and the God who had brought about humanity's rejection. This led him to conclude that this good and excellent God of the gospel could not be the Creator. Thus he posited a second god, a judicial and harsh god, who had created the world. It was a very thin line between Marcion's divorce of the redeeming God and of creation, and the gnostic heresy's teaching that spirituality (*gnosis*) can only be achieved by avoiding the evils of fleshly existence. In fact the Gnostics made this point by drawing upon a distinction between the supreme God and the Creator God.[8]

Although Marcion did not take quite so negative a stance towards creation, it is clear that a separation of the God who sent Jesus Christ from the creation led to a serious deprecation of creation in both movements. For the Gnostics especially, fleshly and material reality was deemed evil. Consequently both had tendencies to be *docetic* (to deny the true humanity of Christ) since a good and holy God could not become incarnate in evil flesh. The church could only respond to these heresies by unambiguously asserting the goodness of creation. (Marcion's separation of the Creator God from the good God of Jesus Christ also led him to disengage the gospel from all Jewish roots, and so from the Old Testament. In reaction to this and to his amending of several New Testament texts, the church was stimulated to establish which books belonged to canonical Scripture.) In like manner the church's insistence that humanity is created in God's image (*imago dei*) was stimulated by a similar challenge to the goodness of creation by the fourth-century dualistic religion Manicheism.[9] This concept of *imago dei* may also serve to account for how humanity, though part of the creation and ultimately connected to it, may also exercise authority over creation. Presumably humans may exercise such authority on behalf of God because we are in God's image (cf. Gen. 1:26).

This reference to the *imago dei* concludes our discussion of the dimensions of the doctrine of creation about which the catholic church has come to agree. However, as with the Trinity and most other doctrines, no formal definition of the concepts associated with the doctrine of creation has ever been ratified. This has resulted in both confusion and theological diversity in the church.

For example, what it means to say that humanity is created

imago dei (in the image of God) remains a controversial matter. Many theologians have defined the image in terms of some characteristic or quality of human nature such as reason, will, linguistic ability, or God-consciousness.[10] In this way the goodness of God's creation can be affirmed even in face of sin. The problem with this view for some theologians is that it is not possible to say that humanity is totally fallen in sin. Insofar as the image of God is understood as an essential human quality or characteristic, it follows that even in sin the image of God cannot be destroyed if humanity is still to remain human. The contrasting view is not to regard the image as a natural human quality, but to regard it as an external calling like love, faith, and the like.[11] The advantage of this approach is that it allows one to affirm the radicality of sin, which destroys the image of God, without implying that the human in sin is not still God's good creation. (On these grounds we still possess all our natural human characteristics, even in sin.) The debate about what is the most adequate way to speak about the image of God goes on. In order that the gospel may be presented in images which communicate it best in our present situation, it is well that this debate continue and that it stimulate the church to further reflection.

There is a second concept related to the early church's treatment of creation about which subsequent Christian theology has not yet come to basic agreement. This is the concept of the natural law of creation, which was used by the church to facilitate dialogue with the non-Christian culture by which it was surrounded. Subsequent history of the church indicates that natural law has played this role by stimulating dialogue with or ethical involvement in the secular realm. The crucial question dividing Christians on the issue has been: what sort of claims can be made on the basis of the natural law? On one side we find theologians who argue that since the natural law is accessible to reason and since the natural law gives witness to God, it is possible to reason to the existence of God through an analysis of the structures of creation.

The *cosmological argument* for the existence of God, which we discussed in a previous chapter, employs this procedure. It is a venerable theological orientation and seems to have some biblical basis (cf. Rom. 1:20–23; Acts 17:22ff.).[12] Many people in our society still do have a sense of God's presence in the natural world. Yet as we noted earlier, philosophical developments since the Enlightenment have called the validity of this argument for the existence of God into some question.[13] For this reason alternative understandings of the natural law in creation have been articulated.

All of these alternatives begin with the insistence that God can be known truly only through Christ (John 14:6). The great concern is that classical arguments for God's existence lead to a kind of naturalism, which compromises the Christian commitment to the centrality of Christ. One response is to regard the natural order as a pointer to God, as a kind of question which can only be answered by God's revelation of himself in Christ. Such a method of correlation or dialectical approach typifies the thought of several twentieth-century theologians like Paul Tillich, Rudolf Bultmann, and Emil Brunner. (In point of fact one must ask whether this approach differs radically from those who opt for the cosmological argument. Even Thomas Aquinas, the foremost proponent of the cosmological argument, presupposed a concept of God given in the Christian tradition.[14] Thus in fact his proof does little more than assert that for Christians creation suggests the existence of God.)

A related, though different, approach is to opt for natural law revealing God when faith is presupposed. Such a view militantly opposes all efforts at correlating knowledge of God and common human experience apart from faith. Yet for the faithful who already know God, all creation is understood as pointing to and confirming God's existence.[15] (This understanding of natural law basically characterizes the perspective of this volume, and it is reflected in the sermon in chapter two.)

The different understandings of the status of natural law which we have considered are perhaps not that distinct. Their differences are significant because of the distinct resources each provides for placing Christianity in dialogue with contemporary culture. However, that consideration cannot be explored in the present work but must be dealt with another day. For the present it is sufficient to indicate that for virtually all Christians, it is not our experience of creation in itself that reveals God to us. Rather, we interpret that experience through the Christ-event.

We have seen that the early church's construction of the doctrine of creation left unresolved questions about the character of the *imago dei* and status of the natural law. The early church was not so ambiguous, however, in the position it took on the relationship between creation and redemption. Nonetheless the nature of this relationship remains a source of great disagreement among theologians.

It has already been noted that the Nicene Creed has implications for understanding how creation and redemption relate. If Christ is of the same substance as the Father so that both he and the Father are agents of both creation and redemption, then it follows that Christ's redeeming work of saving humanity from the nonbeing of sin must be related in some way to his work in creating life out of nothing. In short it seems to follow from such Trinitarian presuppositions that redemption is an instance or intensification of God's ongoing creative activity in making life from nothing (even from the nothingness of sin).

This kind of continuity between creation and redemption has been widely accepted by subsequent theologians. One of its advantages is that it allows Christians to see a continuity between Old and New Testaments. Both give testimony to God's ongoing work in creation. Also the universalist thrust of the gospel can in this way be affirmed (cf. 2 Cor. 5:19; 1 John 2:2). If Christ's work is an instance of God's ongoing creative work and inasmuch as creation has a universal thrust, then Christ's redemptive work must also have this same universal thrust and be for the whole world.

Despite its strengths, this understanding of the relationship between creation and redemption has been challenged by alternative views. One approach has been to embrace this continuity between creation and redemption in such a way that the fall is taken into account as a necessary part of the creative process. For liberal theologians like Friedrich Schleiermacher and Paul Tillich who take this view, God created the world in such a way that the fall was an unavoidable necessity, so that Christ might come to redeem humanity.[16] This is a comforting perspective insofar as it allows the Christian to affirm that God is in control of the entire process of salvation. Yet questions might be raised about its adequacy for representing the biblical narrative or the radical newness of the gospel (cf. Matt. 9:17; 2 Cor. 5:17; Heb. 8:13). In response, yet a third way of dealing with the relationship between creation and redemption has appeared. In this model, creation and redemption are placed in opposition to each other.

John Calvin and portions of the theology of Martin Luther opt for this kind of approach. The distinction between law (the condemning function of the Word of God) and gospel (its unconditional gift character) implies that God's work in creation must be distinguished from his work in redemption. This manifests itself in the affirmation of double predestination often made by both men. According to this view God only elects some portion of humanity and condemns the remaining portion. On this basis it follows that Christ's redeeming work can only be for the sake of that portion of humanity whom God has elected. Thus redemption does not possess the universal thrust of creation. In that sense it is a new and distinct work of God.

It must be conceded that such a way of relating or distinguishing creation and redemption has difficulties dealing with the universalist thrust of certain portions of the biblical witness. As we have seen it also seems to run counter to the logic of the church's credal formulations. Yet we must respect such a treatment of this issue if for no other reason than the fact that it is a position held by several distinguished members of the Christian family. For the purpose of asserting the radical newness of Christ's redeeming work and protecting the gospel from legalist abuse (so that it is not interpreted in relation to the law of creation), the distinction of creation and redemption must be deemed a valid Christian viewpoints.

This discussion of the relationship between creation and redemption pertains to the question of who the gospel is for—all creation or the elect few. We are thus brought to consider the problem of election. We can conclude this chapter with a brief discussion of the topic.

The concept of *election* is a central biblical theme. Israel is identified as God's elect (Isa. 14:1; Isa. 45:4; Rom. 11:28). The early Christians understood themselves as the elect of God (Rom. 8:33; 1 Thess. 1:4; 1 Peter 1:2). The concept of election refers to the gift of special grace given by God to a certain group of people. With this gift comes both special privileges and special responsibilities. Those who are elect are called to participate with God in God's work in the world. Because of this intimate connection between election and God's ongoing creative work in the world, I have chosen to examine election in the context of this discussion of creation.

Election should be distinguished from *predestination*. Predestination is a subcategory of election. It refers to the special grace given to the elect which brings about their salvation.

Several different approaches to predestination have been adopted in the church. They are helpful to consider at this point because they provide some bearings by which the questions, "Who is the gospel for and who is God working through?" can be answered.

We have previously discussed the notion of *double predestination*. An advantage of this view is that God's omnipotence, God's full control over matters that pertain to salvation and grace, is unambiguously asserted. Thus it is not surprising that historically this view has been taken by theologians when they sought to overturn tendencies to compromise the Pauline commitment to the primacy of grace by certain works-righteous proponents (cf. Rom. 3:24). The problem with such a view is that it presents a very menacing, almost unlovable God. The certainty and security of the gospel is compromised because I can never be sure that Christ is for me. I might be one of the reprobate.

One response to this view has been to deny predestination, as the Methodist reformer John Wesley did.[17] Another problem with predestination, Wesley and Baptist forerunners argued, is that it can undercut the moral life. The potential danger in repudiating the doctrine outright is that the role of the human will can receive such undue emphasis that grace is compromised. This is clearly not a problem in Wesley. Yet it is more of a problem for those who embrace his commitments than for theologians relying on some form of predestination.

Another way of modifying the terrors of double predestination was proposed by certain seventeenth-century Protestant Orthodox theologians. They argued that predestination happens "in view of faith" (*intuitu fidei*). God elects a portion of humankind on the basis of divine foreknowledge of whether or not they will believe.[18]

Such a view may have biblical warrant (cf. Rom. 8:29). Yet it is less certain that it adds much to Wesley's rejection of predestination. The great danger in this view is that it might imply that believers, not God determine who is elect. The comfort that is given in knowing that election is not my responsibility may be compromised.

Who is the gospel for? Who is to participate in God's work? The final two alternatives take with utmost seriousness the universal thrust of certain New Testament pericopes (cf. Rom. 11:26; 2 Cor. 5:19; 1 Tim. 2:4; 1 John 2:2). The first of these is an outright affirmation of universal salvation (*apokatastasis*), the salvation of all creatures. This view was principally held by third-century church Father, Origen.[19] This is a majestic and comforting vision. Yet it is difficult to reconcile this view with Scripture's references to hell and a final judgment (cf. Rev. 20:13–15). Thus many Christians, especially Lutherans, have opted for a *single predestination*.

Single predestination posits that election is God's work but that this only pertains to God's chosen children. Those who do not come to faith or belong to the kingdom have only themselves to blame. Failure to be included among the elect is the unbeliever's fault.[20]

This approach to the problem bears the burden of implying a paradoxical position. If God elects does God not by implication condemn those who are not chosen? The only way to render this view intelligible seems to be to argue that the gospel is for everyone, that all are elect. Yet some have rejected this election by willful disobedience and hardheartedness (cf. Matt. 12:31; Luke 12:10). The tension between Scripture's universalist thrust and its witness to a final judgment can in this way be maintained. Of course the question of how we can reject what God has given us or of how faith can be both our work and God's work in us is a matter which deserves further clarification. This will be offered in the chapter on the Holy Spirit. For the present it is sufficient to observe the great comfort believers may have in knowing that God has chosen them through God's electing grace alone, not on account of what they have done.

The sermon which follows in this chapter will implicitly draw upon the notion of single predestination. The universalist thrust of this idea correlates with the belief that all are elect in some sense through creation. (This provides further rationale for why I have dealt with election under the rubric of creation.) This means that all are elect for we all bear the image of God.

The sermon will extrapolate these concepts by interpreting the image, not as some natural human characteristic, but as an external calling. The special task or calling to which we are elected is understood as the call to participate in God's ongoing creative work (cf. Ps. 104). We are in God's image to the extent our capacities are used in creating good. As such, our purpose in life is intimately connected with what is good for the whole creation, not just with narrow human aims. To be in God's image is to be "ecological creatures."

Such a treatment of these concepts of election and *imago dei* implies that a continuity of creation and redemption is assumed in the sermon. To speak of participating in God's creative projects means that creation is an ongoing process and not only a past event. (Thus redemption must be an instance of creation.) This is among the most profound insights the Christian doctrine of creation can offer to our daily lives. The sermon tries to show the peace of mind and sense of purpose given to us when we know God is still active in creation and in all things working for good. Christians have a sense of purpose for they have been elected to work with God on behalf of creation. To know the doctrine of creation is to affirm the goodness of life and to work in its behalf.

§

Text: Psalm 104
(*Preached in urban congregation.*)

"What makes the world like it is? What is our purpose in the world?" The psalmist has an answer to these questions for us. The world is like it is because of God and God's ongoing involvement in it. And the fact that the world is God's says something about what our purpose in it is. Our purpose in life, we are told in this psalm, is intimately connected with the rhythms and living things which comprise planet Earth. Thus without an appreciation of creation we can never get a true sense of meaning and purpose in life. The doctrine of creation is an essential ingredient in coming to know who we are. This morning let's talk about this and see what we can learn from the psalmist.

The doctrine of creation: this has been a very controversial matter for Christians at least since the nineteenth century, if not before. Did God create the world in seven days? Can we trust the historical truth of the Genesis accounts of creation? What are we to make of Charles Darwin's theory of evolution and modern archaeological discoveries? They seem to call the credibility of the biblical accounts into question. These have been poignant questions for the church. They are questions with which most of us here today struggle. What does the Christian doctrine of creation have to say to twentieth-century people with our modern scientific world view?

First, let me tell you what I am *not* going to do today. I am not going to attempt to defend the Genesis account from scientific criticism, nor do I plan to propose a way of synthesizing the creation narrative and evolutionary theory. I believe that in the past we have spent so much time trying to discover an intellectually credible way of "solving the problem" of creation that we have tended to ignore the very valuable significance of creation for our everyday lives. Let me spell that out a little bit more.

I would not be telling you any secret by saying that we live in a time when God seems far away. Christian faith seems like an irrelevant vestige of the past to so many. Even we in the church sense a kind of distance from God. We typically think of God as "out there," removed from our daily lives. Correspondingly, this sense of God's absence has led to a loss of meaning and purpose in life for many in our society. People are madly searching for a sense of who they are. "I've gotta get my act together" is a commonly heard lament. Let me suggest to you, my friends, that these attitudes are connected with, are symptoms of, the fact that the creation doctrine has lost its significance for us.

This brings us back to the problem we were examining earlier. Our concern to discern an intellectually credible view of creation has led us to compromise the significance of the doctrine for our lives. Let me illustrate this with a question: when I talk about creation, what is the first image that comes to your mind?

For some of us, awe and wonder would certainly be components of our reaction. Betsey, Pat, and I spent the summer in the West, visiting the great national parks and soaking up the stunning scenery. You just can't help but marvel at the earth, its richness and variety, its beauty. Yet the tragedy is that we do not stop and take note of this most of the time. Rather when we think of creation we are more apt to take it for granted and to assume its predictability. That is not surprising. Intimately bound up with the view of creation most of us have is the idea of nature's laws. I'll bet this was the image that came to most of you when I asked you to think of an image to describe creation. Am I correct? We typically think of creation as having been structured in such a way that we know what to expect from it. Seasons change, the sun rises and sets, objects fall on account of gravity. Creàtion is seen as a kind of giant mechanical system. It is no wonder we tend to neglect its beauties and forget to stop and smell the roses. In our mechanized daily lives, creation seems just one more machine.

This idea of creation as a kind of smooth-running watch is really the fruit of efforts to make the idea of creation credible in the modern world. About three hundred years ago as advances in science began making the idea of God's direct intervention in the world less credible, the idea of God as a master clock-maker, who made the world perpetually to tick away smoothly by itself, was developed. The name of this view of creation is deism. Deism is the idea that God created the world with certain natural laws. These laws govern creation so perfectly that now it runs by itself without needing God.

Does this sound familiar? It should. Many of us have grown up with this idea of deism. I know I did. It was taught in the schools indirectly as part of our national religious spirit. That is not surprising since our founding fathers were quite influenced by deism.

Given the dominance of this way of looking at creation in our society, it is little wonder that a sense of God's distance from the world has been reinforced. No wonder we have difficulty integrating our Christianity with our daily lives. No wonder God does not seem present with us in our homes, with our families, or on the job. God is removed from our lives; God is just letting the world "do its thing." This pretty well summarizes our outlook on creation and our sense of God's involvement in our daily lives, does it not? It also accounts for the lack of a sense of purpose in life which many of us feel. The world is just another machine which functions as our master or our slave. Life means functioning as an operator of that machine, with no more sense of purpose than any machine operator in mass production feels. The image of creation as a machine, with no apparent purpose beyond maintaining itself, merely reinforces the feeling that life is a meaningless rat race.

Is that all there is to life? What are we doing here? These are the questions we asked at the beginning of the sermon. In answering these questions the psalmist says:

> Bless the LORD, O my soul! . . .
> Thou makest springs gush forth in the valleys
> they flow between the hills,
> they give drink to every beast of the field; . . .
> Thou dost cause the grass to grow for the cattle
> and plants for man to cultivate,
> that he may bring forth food from the earth.
> (Ps. 104:1, 10–11, 14)

The God of the psalmist is not a mere clock-maker, who sits back and lets creation "do its thing." This is a God who is still engaged in the process of making living things grow, a God who actually feeds and waters them. This is a God who is still active and still meddling in creation. To a world in which God seems so distant and irrelevant the psalmist's picture provides a genuine alternative. If we want to know where God is and what God has to do with our daily lives we need only stop and reflect on all the good things we have been given. Our bodies, all our rational facilities, our food, clothing, home, family, all the necessities of life are evidences of God's involvement in our existence.

This is not to say that God can be known through creation without reference to Jesus Christ. Because of the ambiguities of life, because of evil, we are unable to discern the love of God in everything that happens in creation. Therefore, we need Jesus and the Word to function as spectacles for discerning the God of love in our world. (This perspective is assumed in the remainder of my comments about creation.) In this understanding of creation Christians have an answer to the first question I raised: what makes the world like it is? The world is like it is, insofar as creation is good, because God is active in it. God is still in the process of creating. (This idea of creation as an ongoing process, coupled with the Mosaic affirmation that this process has a point of initiation, may provide some clues for constructing a proposal which integrates the creation narratives with evolutionary theory. If the Christian community has a biblical basis for understanding creation as an ongoing process there is certainly legitimation in interpreting evolutionary theory in light of God's ongoing work of creation.)

This appreciation of creation has an even more relevant contribution to make to our daily lives. It provides us with a sense of purpose, a sense of what we are all about. Paul gives us the nicest summary of this purpose. He wrote: "We know that in everything God works for good with those who love him, who are called according to his purpose" (Rom. 8:28). In everything God works for good. We have here in a nutshell God's purpose in creation. In all God does God is working to create new good (cf. Ps. 145:9–10).

The recognition of this purpose in creation gives genuine comfort. What happens in life is not chaos. The order inherent in creation and our world is not that of a machine working aimlessly. The cycles of life are not meaningless. There is a purpose in the change of seasons, in the growth process, in the rain and sun; there is even purpose in my daily work. God is working through them to create new good in the creation.

This gives us some clues about the meaning and purpose of our lives. The biblical witness reports that human beings have been chosen by God, elected by God, to share in the ongoing process of creating new good. (When Paul talks about election in Romans 8:29 he says the elect are conformed to Christ. What else can this mean but that election entails sharing in Christ's ongoing work of creation? God's command to humanity in Genesis 1:28 to subdue the earth also suggests that we have been called to work with God in creating and cultivating the earth.) We have a task, friends, something to *do* with our lives. In all our activities we are people whom God intends to use in creating new good.

In our time, when life seems aimless for many people and when so many are seeking for meaning and purpose, our text and the Christian doctrine of creation has a very relevant and comforting message; creation has a purpose. God is using it to work good.

Stop and smell the roses, friends! The world and its natural phenonema are not accidental existences meaningful only insofar as they serve us. No, the world and its natural phenomena are expressions of the good which God is still creating. Celebrate it, and revel in the beauty and goodness of what God has done.

More than that, the doctrine of creation points us to our purpose as creatures. As we marvel at what God has done in this world we may begin to appreciate how good and beautiful we are. For you and I are part of God's good creation. We are beautiful! Feel good about yourself.

The doctrine of creation, though, implies that what we are and have today is only the beginning. We have a future and a purpose. God intends that we use ourselves, our talents, and the world not to our own selfish advantage. Rather, our purpose is to use our talents to subdue the earth, in order to join with God in creating good in it. God would have us and our world be better than we already are. That is good news, friends! Who says the gospel is not found in the Old Testament? What the doctrine of creation says to us in our search for meaning and purpose is very good news indeed. Amen.

Chapter Five
SIN

The church did not develop a doctrine of sin until relatively late. It is not surprising that the church did not hasten to clarify its understanding of sin in view of the negative tones set by the doctrine. Whether it be the first century or today, human beings have never been particularly open to a way of viewing themselves which might undercut a sense of human dignity and humanity's infinite possibilities. Yet, in fact, the real reason the doctrine of sin was a relatively late product of the early church was not because of the pessimistic attitude associated with it. Rather the church's deliberateness on the question of sin was a result of the doctrine being formulated only as a consequence of the church's understanding of salvation and its practice of infant baptism.[1] Such an observation makes good sense. Only after the church had clarified for itself the meaning of Christ's redemptive work could it begin to understand the malady which salvation had cured. In like manner the problem of sin (specifically original sin) did not preoccupy the church until it was necessary to offer justification for the practice of infant baptism. If all humans exist in a state of sin and none are innocent, then it becomes necessary to baptize all, even infants, in order that they might be saved from sin.

This latter insight was first articulated by the third-century North African Bishop Cyprian. In earlier centuries Christians had been less concerned to assert sin's inevitability in this way. Rather it was more important to assert human responsibility for sin in face of the determinism of much hellenistic philosophy. Thus theology done prior to the Council of Nicea tended to emphasize human free will. The break with this pattern, first occasioned by the infant baptism issue, was more fully developed by the great fifth-century theologian St. Augustine.[2] His more complete development of the doctrine of sin was occasioned by the Pelagian controversy and the evolution of his own theology.

Pelagianism was a fourth- and fifth-century heresy which taught that human beings have a will free to choose between sin and perfection. As such, grace was helpful, but not necessary, for living the Christian life. Such a view was directly counter to Augustine's commitments to humanity's complete dependence on grace and the sovereignty of God.[3] These commitments led him to assert a doctrine of double predestination (cf. chapter four). In this way it could be soundly asserted that salvation is totally the work of grace and not dependent on human merit. It was here that the notion of original sin's further development played an important role. Augustine was enabled to proclaim humanity's absolute dependence on grace because he came to understand all humanity as fallen and sinful, unable to come to God of its own volition.[4] Original sin was asserted to explain how all people had fallen into this sinful condition. This seemed like a valid conclusion inasmuch as the New Testament hinted about the concept of sin being transmitted to all humanity through Adam (cf. Rom. 5:12–14; 1 Cor. 15:22).

Pelagianism with its optimistic view of human nature called this into question. In a subsequent chapter more details will be provided on the issues at stake in this controversy. For the present suffice it to say that the Pelagian controversy provided Augustine further opportunity to formalize his thoughts on grace, predestination, and original sin. Ultimately the church supported Augustine. It condemned Pelagius at the Council of Ephesus in 431, and in so doing, not only supported Augustine's insistence on the necessity of grace for salvation, but also affirmed the doctrine of original sin. Subsequently this doctrine and the core of Augustine's theology of grace (with the exception of his double predestination) were reaffirmed by the Synod of Orange in 529. The doctrine of sin and original sin was now firmly in place.[5]

These historical considerations about the development of the doctrine of sin teach us an important lesson in regard to how we should deal with it. Just as the early church could not come to an understanding of sin before it gained clarity about the nature of salvation and baptism, so contemporary Christians ought not deal with sin apart from or prior to these topics. In some respect, then, the order of consideration of topics in this volume is misleading. Sin cannot be rightly understood apart from the gospel. Thus the analysis of the doctrine which follows should be understood as presupposing an understanding of Christ, his atoning work, and justification (i.e., the content of the next three chapters).

The Christian understanding of sin involves at least two components: (1) human responsibility for sin and (2) an affirmation of its inevitability.[6] The latter component is upheld by the doctrine of original sin. Thus it follows that sin can never be understood solely in terms of specific acts which are contrary to the law of God. Sin is a state or situation which permeates all that human beings do. We can appreciate this more fully once we have further elaborated the Christian understanding of persons.

We noted in the preceding chapter the church's commitment to affirming the goodness of creation and the goodness of humanity. Yet the doctrine of sin affirms that since the fall, humanity is *totally* immersed in sin (though not at the expense of undoing the goodness of creation). The question then becomes how this can be asserted by Christians who believe that human beings possess an everlasting soul. Such an entity could not by definition be tainted by sin because it remains in eternal fellowship with the infinite God. In fact this is no problem for Christian faith because the idea of an everlasting soul is an extraneous element to Christianity. Thus a brief digression to make this point more fully is warranted.

The "popularized" understanding of the Christian view of personhood as an eternal soul implanted in a body is in fact a gnostic belief. We have already noted in the preceding chapter that *gnosticism* was a dualistic redemption-religion which invaded hellenism from the Orient. It posited that humanity's heavenly element, the soul, was imprisoned in the body. The widespread acceptance of this view of persons in the hellenistic period is not surprising in view of its proximities to the body/soul dualism of classic Greek philosophers like Plato.

At any rate this view of persons was so embedded in the culture of the first century Near East that its concepts permeated the vocabulary of the Apostles. Without employing these concepts the proclamation of the early church would have been incomprehensible to the wider culture. Thus we may discern several instances where the language of body/soul dualism appears in the New Testament (cf. 1 Cor. 7:34; 1 Thess. 5:23). In the same manner Christian theologians throughout history, largely because of the great influence of Greek thought on western civilization, have developed the Christian view of persons in terms of this body/soul dualism.[7] It is little wonder this view has been so indelibly stamped on the piety of many Christians. In fact, however, the biblical writers did not appropriate this notion of an eternal soul uncritically. Rather such language was employed, but its meaning was subtly redefined to fit the hebraic view of persons.

The Old Testament clearly knows no body/soul dualism. Its basic anthropological concept is the Hebrew word *nephesh*, which translates literally "breath" or "life." This breath of life given by God is what constitutes a human person as a psycho-physical self(cf. Ps. 97:10; 104:29–30, 35). Yet as the first biblical reference to humanity makes clear there is no life (*nephesh*) apart from the body (Gen. 2:7). (It should be noted at this point that the Revised Standard Version does translate *nephesh* as "soul" on occasion. Yet these references cannot properly be equated with the hellenistic/gnostic notion of an eternal soul which exists independent of a body. No distinction between one's psycho-physical self, one's vitality, and one's body is meaningful on these grounds. Lev. 17:11: "For the life of the flesh is in the blood.") This is precisely the view of persons appropriated by the New Testament authors, who reinterpret the concepts associated with the gnostic view in this light.

Such a reinterpretation process is evident in several places where Paul attributes to the body certain spiritual characteristics more properly identified on gnostic suppositions with the soul (cf. Rom. 6:1; Rom. 12:1; 1 Cor. 6:19). As in the Hebrew view, the functions of the soul and even the soul itself seem to have no independent status on these grounds. This is most clearly affirmed by a fundamental credal statement, "the resurrection of the body" (1 Cor. 15:25; cf. Isa. 26:19). There is no eternal life apart from the body. The Christian view of persons, then, is radically distinct from the "popular," gnostic idea of the eternal soul in a body. Rather, for Christians a soul independent of a body is an empty, impossible thing. The biblical soul/body language is merely a kind of logical distinction between one's self-conscious and physical dimensions. Yet the two are so inseparably connected that the whole person, both the self-conscious (soul) and physical (body) dimensions, is affected by what happens to either. With this understanding of the Christian view of persons in hand it is possible to see why sin corrupts the *whole* person. Nothing, not even the soul, is left untouched by sin.

Returning now from our digression to consideration of the nature of sin, it must be conceded that Christians have not achieved much consensus about the doctrine beyond affirming the dual components of human responsibility for sin and sin's inevitability. Various master images (ego, pride, selfishness, sloth, disobedience, unfaith, idolatry, inauthenticity, etc.) have been employed to describe sin. All of them share a common idea expressed by the Greek term *hamartia*—"missing the mark." Sin is a missing of the mark set by God, not merely a sense of anxiety or dissatisfaction with oneself. We only know sin as an offense against God and God's will. Additionally when any of these master images are employed for describing sin they must be used in such a way that they do not merely connote temporary attitudes, but rather a whole mode of existence in which humans are trapped (i.e., the inevitability of sin). To the degree they convey the idea that sin is out of control, bigger than the individual, we can begin to relate the doctrine of sin to the biblical image of the devil. This kind of relationship between sin and the forces of evil is a very important consideration for certain understandings of the atonement (see chapter seven).

Such master images must also convey one other dimension: the idea that humans have been blinded to God by the characteristic in question. As long as a given image conveys these dimensions of inevitability and offense against God, the Christian is free to employ whichever images seem most appropriate for relating the doctrine of sin to contemporary situations. In our time and place selfishness and self-preoccupation probably do this as well as any image.

There are some issues, though, about which Christians disagree more substantially than they do in regards to the core image for describing sin. One of these areas of disagreement was touched on in the preceding chapter—the question of the status of the image of God. We noted then that some theologians understand the *imago dei* to refer to some characteristic or quality of human nature. The problem with such a view is akin to that of the idea of an eternal soul. It implies that there is something in a human person (this characteristic or quality) which is "unfallen," since to the extent one still has this quality or characteristic, he or she is still in God's image (and so unfallen). By contrast a second way of talking about the image of God is to regard it as an external calling like love, involvement in God's creative projects, or the like. On these grounds one is better able to affirm the totality of sin.

One final issue to be considered, which has further divided theologians, is the question of how to relate human responsibility for sin with sin's inevitability. Some theologians of the early church like the fourth-century Bishop of Milan, Ambrose, and St. Augustine, (largely through the influence of a growing asceticism) spoke of the sexual transmission of original sin. The development of a doctrine of the virgin birth, correlated with the affirmation of Jesus' sinlessness, further enhanced this belief. Those theologians maintained that original sin is transmitted to all (we are born in sin) because we are products of sinful lust and sexual intercourse.[8]

This understanding of the sexual character of sin's transmission remains very influential in the church today. Such a view clearly affirms sin's inevitability. It is less clear that it accounts for the individual's responsibility for sin. Its negative evaluation of sexuality must also be examined critically in view of the biblical affirmation of creation's goodness and the apparent affirmation of sexual procreation (Gen. 1:28, 31; 1 Tim. 4:4). An alternative proposal for dealing with the relationship between sin's inevitability and human responsibility for sin has been proposed by more modern theologians like Karl Barth. His is basically the perspective of this volume.

Like Barth we begin by affirming that Adam's original sin is our sin. Thus each individual is responsible for sin insofar as all have repeated Adam's sin.[9] The problem for this view is how to assert sin's inevitability if original sin is not inherited but repeated by each individual. The answer is to be found in the view of personal identity articulated in the first chapter. There it was noted that human identity is not innate in persons, but instead is shaped by all the things they have done or experienced. This would mean that a person who came into contact with nothing but sinful people would *inevitably* sin. If sin is done to me by others, it constitutes my identity as a sinner; thus I shall inevitably sin.

On these grounds sin is inevitable because of the sinful company we keep—what is done to us. Yet we are still responsible for our sin, just as we are responsible for our decision to affirm democratic processes even though virtually everyone we know accepts democracy as a good thing. Just as it is really you who affirm the democratic process even though you inevitably make this affirmation because you are so heavily influenced, so you are responsible for sin. As long as human responsibility and sin's inevitability are both affirmed the precise nature of how they are related is indifferent.

The doctrine of sin does undercut exalted optimism about human nature and its capabilities, but perhaps it is not as pessimistic a view of reality as might appear at first glance. It clearly makes important contributions to an understanding of life. It lends a touch of realism to our expectations of others, ourselves, and the world. This is a particularly important contribution for us living in a world where once-great hopes for the future are not being realized as the old social order gradually deteriorates. In a related manner, this doctrine allows us to interpret our world and the evils in it. Not that evil and death should be explained in terms of scientific causality in relation to sin. Yet the doctrine does allow Christians to affirm the goodness of God's creation in face of evil and death. They cannot be deemed God's doing by anyone who has an awareness of sin. Rather evil and death are understood by Christians to have come into the world only because of sin (Rom. 6:23; cf. Gen. 2:17; Rom. 5:12; James 1:15).

In addition to this kind of realism, which ensues when we come to know ourselves as we really are, the doctrine of sin offers yet one more contribution to the Christian life. It provides us with a sense of our limits and so our complete dependence on Christ and his work. The following sermon makes this point. Sin is understood in the sermon principally in terms of a selfish, egocentric use of the creative capacities given us by God. Our responsibility for sin and its inevitability are affirmed.

§

Text: Genesis 2:7–9, 15–17; 3:1–7
(Preached in rural congregation.)

Let me tell you, my friends, the lessons which have been assigned by the lectionary for this year are genuine challenges. Take this morning's as an example. How can you preach a sermon on the third chapter of Genesis, the story of the fall? Who believes in original sin these days?

Original sin: what do you think about it? do you believe in it? On account of Adam's sin all human beings are placed under the sentence of eternal damnation! Not one of us, not even a little baby, is free from sin. We are all scarred, marred, and going to hell—all because of Adam.

For many people original sin connotes all this. Yet it does not seem right. Why should all of us poor innocent people in this parish be punished just because Adam blew it? It is not fair!

If this is what original sin is all about, who needs it? At any rate, this is the way a lot of Christians feel. We protest that human beings cannot be entirely rotten, that we are able to do *some* good things. Little babies cannot be sinful, we argue. And why should we all be punished because of Adam? Who cares about original sin? Who needs it?

The doctrine of original sin: do we Christians need it? if so, how come? what is its significance? I hope you have asked these questions, at one time or another because that is what the rest of this sermon is all about. Paul and I are going to try to convince you all just how important it is for us Christians to believe in original sin.

First, let me give you a warning. I am a bit prejudiced on this one. I have always been known among my fellow pastors and fellow students as a big "sin" man. I have been accused of being a real pessimist when it comes to human nature, and I believe I am faithful to the biblical witness in this respect. I think I can show that the idea of original sin is present in our first two lessons this morning (Gen. 3:1–7; Rom. 5:12–19). There is no way of avoiding this doctrine. One cannot call oneself Christian and not struggle with the idea of original sin. Since it is that important, I should start trying to explain what original sin really is. Let's give it some thought together.

The doctrine of original sin is really saying to us, "Look, people, there is not a thing in life that is not spoiled by sin. There is not a single person, not a single deed you and I can do, not a single thing on this earth that is not tinged with sin." Perhaps this sounds too harsh to you, but it all makes a lot of sense to me. It makes a lot of sense when I think about my life and the things I do. Join me, and take a serious look at your own life right now.

Be honest with yourselves, friends. Is there *anything* in your life, *anything* you do, that is not tinged with sin, even if just a little? Not so fast with your answer now. Think about it. I want you all to think about one of your good deeds, one of the good things you have done lately. Give it some thought, and I'll bet you will feel good as you reflect on your good deed. But the question is: were you really serving God, really serving your loved ones? Or were you in reality serving yourself and your ego? I know I must plead guilty.

This selfishness surfaces in the most innocent ways. It even appears sometimes in our parish on Sunday morning in the sermon. I am not proud to admit it, but there are some Sundays when it is more important to me that you think my sermon is good than that what I say really serves God. Thus even preaching a Christian sermon, a sermon all about God, is tinged with sin and selfishness.

I speak the harsh truth at this point. There are no good deeds that are not tainted by sin. Why? Because we do them selfishly.

Even our best acts, even our service to God is motivated, though unconsciously, by the desire for our own good. All our good deeds are touched by this selfishness, by our sin.

For instance, if I buy Betsey a super Valentine's Day present am I *really* doing it for her? Yes, in part. Yet if I get that present for Betsey, is not part of the reason because then I can say to myself: "Oh, Mark. Boy, you're a *great* husband." Does this sound familiar to you? I'll bet it does. Selfishness: all our good deeds are somewhat spoiled by selfishness, by our sin.

I hope you have all noticed that I have been talking about sin and selfishness as if they were the same thing, and when it comes to original sin they are virtually identical. This is evident in the account of the fall. God had established human beings as partners with God in the care and maintenance of the earth (Gen. 1:26). But we (Adam and Eve) were not content with this particular form of partnership, as impressive as it might seem. We wanted more. As did Adam and Eve in the story, we continue to exercise our jurisdiction over the earth in a way that pleases us, even if it is contrary to God's plan. We use our power over the earth to please ourselves. We assert our own priorities, grab for our own desires, and in so doing we forfeit God's creative purpose for us. We take God's good gifts and the good God works through us, and we use it to serve our own selfish aims. We are all guilty; we have all fallen in sin.

My poll would pertain to infants as well: yes, even sweet innocent little babes. After all, what is more selfish than a little baby? I love our son Pat, but like any infant, if he doesn't get his way, he pouts. That is the point of the doctrine of original sin. It informs us that there is no one who is not hung up on selfishness. Even in the good things we do it's "Me and my projects first"—God and everybody else second. If you are honest with yourself, I think you will admit how snugly the shoe fits. Original sin really does make sense, doesn't it?

We human beings are in quite a jam, what with our selfishness lousing up all our good deeds so that are are unable to do anything that is perfect. It is quite a jam. Yet we cannot blame it all on Adam even though we might like to. Of course he is represented as the first of us human beings to blow it. As Paul says, sin came into the world through Adam (Rom. 5:12). Yet just the same, the blame is not all Adam's. For we can find ourselves in Adam. All of us here in this place are living our lives in sin just like he did. The Hebrew term "Adam" suggests this. The term translates "man" which suggests Adam represents us all. Adam is certainly not the only sinful human being in history. We are all misappropriating God's good gifts, just as he did.

The relationship between Adam's sin and ours has been nicely described by one of my favorite Christian theologians, who said: "We all live our lives repeating Adam's decision, disobeying God and indulging our selfishness."[10] No, we cannot blame it all on Adam. It is our own selfishness, our own needs to to get a pat on the back and have things our own way, which have frustrated God's purpose for the world. It is our own fault we find ourselves in the middle of sin and selfishness.

This is certainly a depressing sermon thus far, is it not? At least it should be. For if I have explained original sin properly to you today, then you ought to be beginning to realize that we can never do anything that is not tinged by sin. We simply cannot avoid sin no matter how hard we try. We cannot cease to be selfish, even when we do good things for our neighbors. Sin is not just breaking the Ten Commandments. Sin is a way of being, a kind of selfishness that intrudes on us even when we keep every one of the Ten Commandments. Even at our very best, we fall short of perfection. Good deeds do not win us any brownie-points; they will not get us to heaven. For they are imperfect; they are tinged with sin.

This is what the doctrine of original sin is all about. Even our good deeds, my friends, are marred by our selfishness and sin. It is not an easy, comfortable insight. Yet it has great significance for us as Christians. Indeed, it is essential for our relationship with God. Why?

First of all, the doctrine is pretty good medicine against our friend, the dreaded disease of "pride-itis." Without the doctrine of original sin we are prone to say, "Look how much better I am than the other people, God." But with it in view we must admit that we are no better than our brothers and sisters. All of us are in the same boat, equally mired in sin.

An awareness of original sin affects us in our life of faith in another way that is perhaps even more important. For we sinful human beings like to forget that we are sinners. We would rather not admit it. Without this doctrine we could all say to God in our own hearts, "Look, God, surely I make my share of mistakes and have my sins, but I make up for it. See how much better I am than that person over there."

The real importance of the doctrine of original sin is that it functions as a constant reminder that we do not get any "brownie-points" with God for our good deeds. Why? Because all those good deeds are tainted by our selfishness and sin. This makes what Jesus Christ did for us all the more important. On account of original sin and our selfishness, God does not owe us anything but damnation. Yet in our helplessness, God died for us. God suffered to save us from the sin which was destroying and distorting us, which was preventing us from sharing in God's eternal project of creating new good in the world (see Col. 2:5).

The doctrine of original sin reminds us how sin and selfishness louse up every part of our lives. When that happens we are inevitably drawn back to what Christ did for us on the cross. His work, which gets the burden of our sinful past off our back, is that much more important.

Thus it is through Christ's triumph on the cross that the doctrine of original sin is transformed into a resource for faith. Such an awareness of sin helps focus our lives all the more on the importance of Christ. It helps to remind us daily that we could never achieve the kingdom of God by earning it through our own good works. We don't really do any good works, and the good news is that we don't have to! God loves and forgives us just as we are. No affirmation of the dignity and infinite possibilities of human nature (and so implicit denial of our sin) can ever surpass the joy of this good news of God's love for us. Amen.

Chapter Six

CHRISTOLOGY

The New Testament clearly portrays Jesus of Nazareth as human. The accounts of his birth from a woman's womb (Luke 2:7), his bodily needs (Luke 26:42–43), his emotional releases (John 11:35), and his death (Mark 15:16ff.) certainly indicate that he is not to be regarded merely as some divine being masquerading in human form. On the other hand, the biblical witness also suggests a special kind of relationship between Christ and the Father (John 17:22). He is eternally with the Father and exercises divine prerogatives (John 1; Luke 5:21). Additionally, if the church is to remain faithful to the Old Testament witness that it is Yahweh who saves his people (Jer. 30:10; 1 Sam. 14:39), it must follow that God was directly and intimately involved in Christ's saving work. Nor could the New Testament language suggesting Christ's bearing of suffering and punishment for our sins (1 Peter 2:23–24; Heb. 2:17–18; Isa. 53:3–5) be accounted for unless Jesus' full humanity was affirmed.

Thus the very nature of the biblical accounts and the oral tradition entailed that the early church must regard Jesus in some way as both God and man. The doctrine of Christ's two natures (divine and human) was developed as an attempt to clarify the sense in which both God and man are part of Jesus' identity. As with the Trinity doctrine, the doctrine of the two natures evolved in response to heretical movements which were perceived as threats to the biblical witness.

Parallels between the Trinitarian and Christological formulations are striking, both in regard to their common substance and their common history. Both formulations are surrounded by a certain degree of interpretive ambiguity. In part this is because as much as the Trinitarian formula, the Christological formulations were only intended to set limits, to delineate the outer bounds of the Christian faith. Finally, both doctrines were developed in response to the same abuses. In fact the Council of Nicea (A.D. 325), the turning point in the development of the Trinity, was convened principally to deal with Christological questions.

In the third chapter we noted that the judgments of the council were largely concerned with Christological matters. Christ was identified as *homoousios* (of the same substance as) with the Father. In so doing the council repudiated Arianism and Sabellianism/modalism. (See chapter three for details on these heresies.) The Arian contention that Christ was a creature needed to be rejected because it would deny God's active role as agent of reconciliation. Arianism implies that humanity (or its representative) redeems itself. Christ the *creature* redeems humanity. For similar reasons the Sabellian/modalist position was found wanting. In addition to its problems in dealing with New Testament texts which appear to subordinate the Son to the Father (Matt. 26:39; Matt. 27:46; Mark 15:34), the modalist denial of a substantial distinction among persons of the Trinity also implicitly denied justification by grace (God's role as sole agent of reconciliation). If Christ and the Father are to be identified so that the Father also suffered and died in Jesus Christ (*patripassianism*), then someone other than God the Father must have raised Jesus from the dead (Acts 4:10; Acts 13:30, 37; 1 Cor. 6:14; 1 Cor. 15:15).

Another factor in the repudiation of modalism was the challenge it posed to the impassibility of God. On modalist grounds God must be subject to change or circumstances, since God could actually die on the Cross. This image of God may be more palatable to the contemporary Christian community, particularly in view of breakthroughs in the interpretation of Scripture. Contemporary theologians have begun to reappropriate Reformation insights about God's intimate identification with humanity, God's mutability (Gen. 6:6; Exod. 32:14), and God's limitedness (Mark 6:5). Such a view of God was philosophically impossible for the early church. Its heavy dependence upon Platonic philosophy entailed that all substance, including divine substance, must be deemed eternal and changeless.

Associated with modalism was the teaching of a Jewish-Christian sect, the Ebionites. On Christological issues they essentially opted for adoptionism. Jesus was deemed to have become Son of God by adoption when he received the Holy Spirit in His baptism (Matt. 3:16–17). This adoptionist view is a logical complement of the modalist position. Some of its practitioners also held that the Spirit left Jesus at his death. This allowed modalists to deal with the question of how the Father might raise Jesus and not be distinct from the Son. The Father could raise Jesus because he had left Jesus at the time of his death. Thus, the Nicene rejection of modalism/Sabellianism also entailed condemnation of the Ebionite/adoptionist position. In view of the arguments noted above which could revitalize modalism and the New Testament texts which do not preclude an adoptionist Christology (cf. Rom. 1:4), the contemporary church needs to reexamine these options. It may be that the Nicene Fathers have precluded them too quickly.

Thus the Nicene council dealt with two potential Christological abuses and went on record saying unambiguously that Jesus Christ is God. Yet this solution raised more questions. They may be summarized as follows: if Jesus is God how can he still be human? Widespread consideration of this question occasioned the emergence of a gnostic-influenced Christological teaching called docetism. Docetism took several forms. All were united by a common commitment to preserve the divinity of Jesus. One of their presuppositions included a negative assessment of fleshly matter. As a result it was unthinkable that God should choose such an abhorrent vehicle as human flesh by which to reveal the deity. The only alternative was to argue that the divine Jesus did not truly possess a human body, but merely took on the appearance of a body. As such Jesus' sufferings could not be regarded as real. (Docetism remains a very common heresy in contemporary popular piety.)

In order to describe the various forms docetism took and the actual development of the two natures doctrine of the Council of Chalcedon (A.D. 451), it is best to sketch the two prevailing orthodox proposals for dealing with the question of how the divine Jesus could be human. One approach may be called *logos Christology*. This view was associated with the theological school of Antioch. Its prime spokesman was Theodore of Mopsuestia. The Antiochenes began their Christological reflections with the Greek philosophical notion of logos which is usually translated as "Word." As we noted in an earlier chapter the concept is more properly understood to symbolize the fact that reality is structured according to a rational plan. The logos embodies this rational structure of reality. This concept had been applied to Christ in the first century, so John 1:14 was a logical starting-point for logos Christology. The notion of the logos' "dwelling" (ἐσκήνωσεν) among us served the Antiochenes' commitment to preserving the distinction between the indwelling logos and the man he had assumed. (When John 2:19 is read in light of the cross, Jesus' reference to the destruction of the Temple may be deemed as support for this commitment. Christ's body is the "Temple" of the logos.) This is not to say that logos Christology entailed a separation of Christ's divinity and humanity. However, its proponents were unwilling to be very specific about the nature of the union between the logos and Jesus' humanity. (The union was not deemed substantial, nor was it viewed as a union analogous to the unity of body and soul.) The distinction was further confirmed by an insistence that in Christ's redeeming work the logos was active and his humanity passive.

The second orthodox alternative basically emerged out of Alexandria in Egypt. This was the view of *hypostatic union*. A principal proponent was Cyril of Alexandria. In contrast to the Antiochenes, Cyril and others stressed the union of the divine and human in Jesus. Although they were willing to speak of Christ's two natures *(hypostases)*, there was a firm insistence that they could not be separated. Christ's humanity was not properly deemed to have a hypostas or nature of its own because it only existed in conjunction with the Word. A logical consequence of the Alexandrian approach to Christology was the notion of the *communicatio idiomatum* (communication of attributes). This notion helps theologians affirm the unity of Christ's two natures because it provides that all pedicates and qualitities which are properly attributed to one of Christ's natures may also be attributed to the other nature. This Christological insight played an important role in the Reformation period, particularly in the thought of Martin Luther. The resources it provides for Christians to talk about the unity of Christ's person makes it helpful for us today. Were it drawn upon more frequently, contemporary Christians would be better able to undercut docetist tendencies and to take the humanity of Jesus more seriously. The *communicatio idiomatum* may also contribute in another way. It could help Christians to speak of God's involvement in human affairs.

The two orthodox approaches to the Christological question provided the framework for subsequent discussion after Nicea. It is not surprising (since heresy may be defined as an undue emphasis on some otherwise orthodox position) that the heretical views which emerged in the period were closely related to the Alexandrian and Antiochene positions.

One post-Nicene development was a kind of docetism espoused by Apollinaris. Although heavily influenced by the Alexandrian theology of the hypostatic union, Apollinaris so emphasized the distinction between the indwelling logos and the human Jesus that he denied a full incarnation. In his view the logos simply replaced the human spirit of Jesus. Christ possessed a human body and soul, yet by implication he could not be deemed fully human since he did not possess a human spirit. In this respect Apollinaris reflected the Alexandrian commitment to the unity of Christ's person. He was able to assert that the two natures could unite without forming a new nature, as happened in subsequent heretical developments inspired by the hypostatic union (cf. Eutyches). The Christology of Apollinaris was condemned at the Second Ecumenical Council held in Constantinople in A.D. 381. His implicit denial of the incarnation warranted rejection for its soteriological consequences. On such docetic presuppositions, God cannot totally have identified with the human condition and borne our sins (or, as the Orthodox churches claim, deified and elevated human nature).

The second post-Nicene Christological heresy was inspired by Nestorius. Nestorius was quite concerned to distinguish the logos from the humanity of Jesus. Like Apollinaris he worried that a stress on unity might lead to viewing Christ as possessing a hybrid third nature (comprised of divine and human natures). His solution was to speak of Christ having two *prosopa*, which may be translated "persons" or "natures." In Christ each retained its own properties; the two natures remained distinct. (The *communicatio idiomatum* is thereby dismissed.) To this point Nestorius was not in disagreement with the Antiochene logos position. His problems come in his inability adequately to describe how the *prosopa* are unified. He speaks of their "voluntary" union, which suggests that the two natures of Christ are morally united in that each shares a common end and works for a similar purpose. We have then no true incarnation but only a good man in whom God dwelt. Soteriological deficiencies similar to the ones we observed in Apollinaris pertain to Nestorius. Given Nestorius' presuppositions, God has not truly participated in the human predicament. Thus it cannot be said that God has borne our sins (or deified our nature). Nestorianism was condemned in A.D. 431 at the Council of Ephesus.

In view of the condemnation of the Nestorian commitment to distinguishing Christ's two natures, the Alexandrian emphasis on the unity of his person gained dominance after Ephesus. As had happened in the past its central commitments were overemphasized and distorted. A principal party in this regard was Eutyches. He so stressed the unity of Christ's person that he completely denied a distinction of natures in Christ after the incarnation. As a result Christ must be identified in terms of a third hybrid substance, a synthesis of the two natures. Again we cannot truly speak of God's identifying with humanity. The Council of Chalcedon A.D. 451 finally condemned Eutyches. (Other views similar to Eutyches were held by several parties of monophysites even after Chalcedon. These heretical movements maintained themselves into the Middle Ages.) It offered the church's definitive statement on Christology. What Nicea was to the Trinity, Chalcedon is to Christology.

The Chalcedonian formulation represents a compromise between the logos Christology and the hypostatic union. It claims to stand in the tradition of the Nicene (and so Trinitarian) formulation. This is evident inasmuch as it repeated the Nicene affirmation that Jesus Christ is *homoousios* (of the same substance as) with the Father. That is, he is true God. The Council then proceeded to affirm his true humanity. He is said to be *homoousios* "with us in manhood, like us in all things except sin."

The compromise character of this statement subsequently becomes evident. The unity of Christ's person, the hypostatic union, was affirmed. By implication the Chalcedonian formula grants a valid role to the *communicatio idiomatum*. Yet although there is this insistence that Christ's two natures cannot be divided, the commitments of logos Christology are also affirmed by Chalcedon. It insists that the two natures are not confused, that their difference is not removed as a result of their union.

This dual emphasis of the Chalcedonian formulation is absolutely essential if the church is to speak properly about the incarnation. Were we not to speak of a union or unity of the divine and human natures in Christ's person there would be no true incarnation. God could not be seen as one who has borne the human condition on behalf of humanity. Yet if the natures are not distinguished, a true incarnation is forfeit. If the divine nature becomes a constituent element in a hybrid substance then it is not truly God who comes to humanity and redeems us.

Despite these most important insights about Christology which the Chalcedonian formula provides, it leaves other important questions unanswered. Like the Trinitarian formulas, the church's Christological statements are sufficiently ambiguous to allow for a variety of interpretations. One crucial unanswered question is the issue of how to describe the union of the two natures intelligibly. How can Jesus be both God and man?

Of the many proposals which have dealt with this question I am attracted to the insights of the twentieth-century theologian, Karl Barth. Barth has influenced the view of human reality which is executed in a systematic fashion in this volume. This view entails the appreciation of the hebraic view that God and persons are not static essences. Rather people are what they do or experience.[1]

This presupposition underlies the sermon on the Trinity in the third chapter. The Trinity may be conceptualized as follows: God is what God does. What God has done is to reveal the Deity in three ways. This threefold revelation must say something about who God is in essential being. Thus the threefold revelation as Father, Son, and Holy Spirit reveals God's being as threefold.

The same presuppositions may be applied to Christology, to the question of Jesus as both God and man. Thus Jesus is human in that he does the things humans do: he is born, he requires bodily nourishment, he dies. (See biblical references on the first page of this chapter.) Yet he is also God insofar as he does the things God does, like forgive sins (Matt. 9:2–5; Mark 2:5–7; Luke 5:20–23) and perform resurrections (John 11:38–44).[2] Thus Jesus' being must be that of a God-man since he performs actions appropriate to both God and human persons. The dual Chalcedonian commitment to assert the unity of Christ's person (with the *communicatio idiomatum*), while distinguishing his divine and human natures, is adequately affirmed with this proposal. Of course the formal nature of the Chalcedonian statement guarantees that Barth's proposal for dealing with the two natures cannot have the final word. Any proposal which respects the twofold Chalcedonian commitment is orthodox.

We have already noted the importance of the Chalcedonian emphasis on the integrity of both of Christ's natures for defending a genuine incarnation. The integrity of the doctrine of the atonement is also at stake in the affirmation of Jesus as both God and man. If he were not God, the doctrine of justification by grace through faith would be undercut. In that case God could not be the sole agent of reconciliation and justification. Presumably, then, justification would also depend on what humans do. If Jesus were not human then God would not have truly identified God with the human condition and borne our sin.

Both of these concerns have important consequences for our everyday life of faith. Persons have a very different outlook on life if they know they are fully accepted by God, regardless of what they do. Likewise they will have a very different relationship to God, a different feeling about God, as a result of knowing that God has shared their experience. This last point is significant because it underscores another dimension of what is at stake for Christian faith in its affirmation of the incarnation. Insofar as Jesus is God with us, it follows that God is only truly known in Jesus (John 14:6). Thus the incarnation is also central to Christian faith in that it is our ultimate access to knowing who God is. God may be known in other ways apart from Christ. We have already noted that some theologians have argued that God may be known in nature or at least that the structure of reality suggests the likelihood of God's existence. Yet the alternative perspective, that these other means of knowledge only make the true God intelligible in light of Christ, seems more persuasive and is less prone to the risk of naturalistic distortion. (See Acts 17:22ff.; Rom. 1:20–23.)

The next chapter on the atonement will further develop these remarks about the significance of the incarnation for Christian faith. However, since the cross and resurrection of Jesus Christ are the heart of Christian faith, we can expect that all doctrines considered will provide further insights about the significance of the incarnation and the doctrine of the two natures for our everyday lives. The following sermon endeavors to offer these kinds of insights. It describes with reference to the circumcision of Jesus the difference an appreciation of *both* Jesus' humanity and his divinity can make in our relationship to God and in our prayer life. The sermon draws very heavily on the *communicatio idiomatum*. The approach is to attribute to Christ's human nature what is properly attributed to his divine nature. Given these presuppositions the incarnation is a doctrine which is highly relevant when facing the ups and downs of daily life.

§

Text: Luke 2:21
(*Preached in rural congregation.*)

There are some real advantages to being a pastor. One of them is that you get to preach almost every week. In what other job do you get about fifteen minutes a week to tell people what is on your mind, even tell them some of your problems?

Today I want to take advantage of this fringe benefit and tell you about a couple of my problems. First, there is one that goes back to my childhood. It has to do with prayer; perhaps some of you have had problems in this area too.

It seems that since childhood everything I learned about Christianity or prayer suggested to me, "Mark, if you have a problem, take it to God." The old hymn always comes to my mind:

> Have we trials and temptations?
> Is there trouble anywhere?
> We should never be discouraged;
> Take it to the Lord in prayer.

Like just about everyone raised in the church, I have been taught that if you have a problem you should take it to God.

There are some problems, though, with this piece of advice: how can we take our problems to God who seems so majestic and far away? How can God understand our problems? I mean, there is God sitting on the heavenly throne in paradise with no problems. How can God understand our problems without ever having had any. How can God really understand what burdens us? God knows about our troubles through omniscience. Yet never having experienced our difficulties and fears, how can God know what they are like?

Of course most of us are willing to accept that through the Bible and through the words spoken by pastors and other members of Christ's body, God can give us advice about dealing with problems. Yet God has never directly dealt with any of them, and as a result Christian advice seems to be cheap advice. It is a bit like the advice given by a teacher or preacher who only possesses "book-learning" and does not have much practical experience. If we do accept such advice, we likely do so only because of our respect for the person. We receive it as advice, not as God's Word. (This may explain why Christian counseling and secular counseling are viewed as interchangeable by many.) God seems very far removed, and laying our problems and fears on God does not seem to offer much comfort. Have you ever felt that way?

My guess is that most of us here today have similar problems with prayer. Since God has not experienced the problems of death, sadness, and loneliness we face, it does not seem that God can understand how we feel. If we feel God cannot empathize or understand, the vibrancy and relevance of Christian faith seems undercut.

So much for my first problem; we will return to it later. Let me now raise another one with you: this week's sermon. Today we celebrate a church festival called "The Name of Jesus." It was formerly called "The Circumcision of Jesus," because tradition holds that eight days after his birth Jesus was circumcised. At that time he received his name (Luke 2:21).

How do you get a sermon out of this topic? Of course Jesus is a nice name, a powerful symbol. In the language that he spoke, Aramaic, the name "Jesus" means "savior." This is interesting and poetic. Yet its significance for us today seems slight.

In my struggles with this topic, it occurred to me that the most recent work our catechical class has been doing is relevant. We have been studying about Jesus Christ and what it means to say he has two natures, that he is both God and man. It strikes me that the fact that Jesus was circumcised says something very important about this doctrine and its relevance for us. It bears on my first problem about prayer. The doctrine of the two natures and Jesus' circumcision presents us with a new picture of God. We meet a God who is with us, who has shared our experience, and with whom we can truly share our burdens.

We must now consider a series of questions: why was Jesus circumcised? what does it say about the doctrine of his two natures? what does it say about God? I shall begin with the first question.

Jesus was circumcised because he was a Jew born of Jewish parents, and in Judaism all males were to be circumcised. Historically the circumcision of males was part of the covenant God made with the Hebrew patriarchs. The covenant made them different, set them apart. The purpose of circumcision, then, was to underline the Jews' separateness. The fact that all Jewish males were circumcised told the gentiles that Jews were different from everybody else. Circumcision for the Jews has certain analogies to Christian baptism; it is the acting out of their belief in God. On the day of circumcision the male child is named in the eyes of God. This is quite appropriate, since on that day he becomes a party to the Jews' covenant relationship with God. As such, the circumcised individual's status also changes in another way. He becomes subject to the law, the Ten Commandments entailed by the Sinai covenant.

It follows, then, that in circumcision Jesus was subjected to the law. In this we have a powerful witness to his full humanity. After all, it is not just the Jews who live under the Ten Commandments. Everybody does; the whole world stands under the burden and the demands of this moral law. All of us feel the need to prove our goodness and our worth.

We all know firsthand that living under the law is not easy. In a way it is impossible, for none of us can follow the Ten Commandments perfectly. The world is not perfect because we all sin. On account of the world's imperfection we all face temptations, trials, sadnesses, and despair.

That Jesus was circumcised is a witness to the fact that he lived under the law and so faced the same problems which confront you and me. His circumcision is not important in itself. It is only important insofar as it testifies to his full humanity, to his facing those same temptations, trials, and pains that we face.

It began with circumcision itself. This is one of the first evidences of Christ's humanity. Jesus experienced the same pain that any male child feels when he is circumcised. It was not just on the cross that Jesus suffered. It happened just eight days after his birth, in circumcision. It was only the beginning for Jesus of the same temptations, same problems that you and I know. As fully human, though, he also experienced some of the same joys that we have felt.

Remember Jesus lived a very routine, humdrum life for a long time. He was not an executive in a big office with high pay and a lot of prestige. He was part of a working family. His father, Joseph, was a carpenter (Matt. 13:55; Mark 6:3). Thus at least indirectly, he experienced the frustrations of work. The New Testament makes it clear that he experienced sorrow and death. We read that he cried bitterly when he learned about the death of his friend Lazarus (John 11:35). Jesus knew what it was to hurt over the death of a loved one.

He also knew about self-doubt (Matt. 4:1–11; Mark 1:12–13; Luke 4:1–13). "What am I living for, God? What am I doing here?"

We all know those questions. We have asked them about ourselves. Careful reading of the Synoptic accounts make it clear that the temptation which Jesus experienced at the beginning of his ministry took the form of questions about the nature of his mission and whether he was in fact the servant of God (the Messiah). We have probably never asked ourselves precisely that kind of question. Yet we have all wondered, "What am I doing here and what is my purpose in life?"

Jesus also sampled the good things in life. It is quite obvious that his affection for and fellowship with his disciples was one of the most beautiful things in his life. (See the sermon in chapter thirteen.) It is evident that Jesus tasted the joy of friendship. He also apparently knew fun and celebration. After all, he performed his first miracle at a wedding (John 2:1–12).

Yet with joy there comes the fear that it will all end someday, the fear of dying. We know very well what happened in Gethsemene. Jesus knew wild fear; he did not want to die (Mark 14:34–36). We also know how he experienced death. Jesus was very much one of us. He was not an angel floating above our human turmoil or some divine being who merely had the appearance of a human. No, Jesus was *completely* human, a man who tasted those same fears, joys, disappointments, and doubts which we all know.

This is the point of Jesus' circumcision, its meaning for us. It says to us that Jesus experienced everything about being human, and if Jesus experienced it, then we can say that God has tasted it too. For God so loved the world that God "emptied himself, taking the form of a servant, being born in the likeness of men" (Phil. 2:7). This is only the case because of the incarnation, since Jesus is both God and human.

The message of Christmas is that God really became human in Jesus Christ. Today the good news is that in the incarnation God has experienced every single dimension of life that we human beings experience, the good and the bad. God is not sitting up in heaven, observing what is happening without really understanding the trials we are going through. Remember that was my first problem with laying my troubles on God.

The meaning of the incarnation, of the two natures doctrine, is that God is just the opposite from the way I had previously thought. God is a God who has been there with us, who has been through it all. Are you down in the dumps, doubting yourself? God knows how that feels. Do you worry about the future? Once God did, too. Are you hurting over the loss of a loved one? In the man Jesus, God grieved. There are few temptations in life which God has not felt. God has been there. That is a pretty good answer to my first problem, isn't it?

God is not really somebody far away. God is not like the chair of the board sitting up in heaven giving orders. Rather, God is very much like a wonderful, sympathetic friend, someone who has been through what we have experienced. Therefore you can lay your problems on God because God has already faced those same problems.

The incarnation enables Christians to make a wonderful claim. We do not pray to a dull, lifeless thing. We pray to a God who has experienced what we experience, who knows what it is like to love and to lose, to fear and to doubt. The words of comfort God speaks to us are not cheap. No, God's Word is the word of experience. That's why we really can "take it to the Lord in Prayer." God has been there and experienced it side-by-side with us as one of us. The story of the circumcision of Jesus and the doctrine of his two natures affirms a vibrant, living, relevant faith. To believe in the incarnation, to say that Jesus is both divine and human, is to know a God who walks, lives, suffers, and rejoices with us daily. Amen.

Chapter Seven

THE ATONEMENT

Jesus' death posed a problem for the early church. There is growing agreement among scholars that the need to explain how and why Jesus had to die stimulated the earliest theological endeavors, even those which shaped canonical texts.[1] Clearly the idea that the Messiah of God had met death on a tree was a source of embarrassment to the early church (cf. 1 Cor. 1:23).

This embarrassment is reflected in the failure of some of the church's earliest theological literature to speak much of the cross and in the tendency to focus instead on Christ's exemplary life. Yet the fact of the cross and its importance for Christian faith was indelibly etched in the early church's life. One finds the language of Christ's sacrificial death and suffering in some early Christian and pre-Christian liturgies.[2] This way of nurturing an awareness of the significance of the cross necessitated further theological reflection about the atonement. Although no formal consensus defining the nature of the atonement has been achieved in the church, it is possible to identify three (and perhaps four) distinct ways in which Christians have explained this doctrine. The following characterization of these ways of talking about the atonement is heavily indebted to Gustaf Aulén's classic book, *Christus Victor*. With the exception of the fourth way of conceptualizing the atonement (a kind of synthesis of the second and third modes), my discussion of the various atonement theories will amount to a brief summary of Aulén's analysis.

The product of the earliest theological reflections on the atonement might be called the *moral influence or subjective theory*. These early theologians understood Christ and his work principally as an example, as the ideal man. His life makes it possible for believers to repent, amend their lives, and so be reconciled to God. There is biblical justification for such a view; Paul calls believers to imitate Christ (cf. 1 Cor. 11:1; Luke 6:36). On these grounds the significance of the cross is somewhat diminished. With the resurrection it is regarded as a kind of seal or vindication of Jesus' teaching, the ultimate expression of God's self-sacrificing love which believers are to imitate.

This way of dealing with the atonement was not just peculiar to early Church Fathers like Cyprian and Clement. It is a theological mode which has been influential in pietism and in the thought of contemporary figures such as Friedrich Schleiermacher, Albrecht Ritschl, Paul Tillich, and other liberal theologians. The strength of this understanding is that it allows a strong emphasis on Christian life, on the appropriation of Christ and his exemplary work. Its problem is that ultimately the atonement is made to depend upon what humans do (albeit with the aid of the Holy Spirit). A more objective approach to the atonement is apparent in the *satisfaction theory*.

Proponents of the satisfaction theory understand Christ's death in terms of a sacrifice. The sacrifice must be offered in order to placate God's wrath against humanity. Sin is understood to have offended God's justice. Because God is just and righteous (cf. Isa. 45:21), sinful humanity cannot be accepted until the debt of sin has been paid. By dying on our behalf Christ wipes away this debt and so restores a right relationship between humanity and God.

This view of the atonement is also biblical (Eph. 5:2; Heb. 10:12). It unambiguously asserts the importance of Christ's death, inasmuch as apart from his sacrificial death humanity is not put right with God. As such the objective character of the atonement is affirmed, since it is in no way dependent on believers as in the moral influence theory. Christ alone atones for sin on our behalf. The only problem with the satisfaction theory is that it can connote a kind of legalism which does not take the radical newness of the gospel seriously. According to this theory God's legal order is not overturned by Christ's work. The law is still the basis for God's relationship with humankind. It is simply that Christ fulfils the law's demands on our behalf.

This legal framework may lead to a tendency to interpret the gospel in light of the law, as manifested in the medieval church's association of this atonement theory with its system of penance (see chapter twelve). Yet the satisfaction theory has had a venerable history of use by the church. It predominated not just in the medieval period but also in Protestant Orthodoxy. One may even discern its influence on early church Fathers like Tertullian and Cyprian, Bishop of Antioch.

Scripture, however, does say more about the atonement with reference to the devil (forces of evil) and Christ's conquering of that which impedes the fellowship between God and human beings (see Col. 2:13–15; Christ's continual confrontation with demons in the Gospels). Those who have been particularly influenced by these passages, men like the second-century Bishop of Lyons, Irenaeus, Martin Luther, and Gustaf Aulén have articulated a third atonement theory called the *classic view*.

The basic thrust of this position is to understand Christ's atoning work as God's victory over the devil and the forces of evil. Even biblical references to the wrath of God (Rom. 1:18; 1 Thess. 2:16) and the law (Gal. 3:13) are interpreted in this scheme. They too are enemies of God against which Christ wins victory. This victory is manifest most clearly in Jesus' resurrection.

Although this dualistic framework of God and evil may at first glance appear mythological and archaic, the classic view has much to commend itself for conceptualizing our understanding of God's redemptive work in our present cultural context. The breakdown of our old societal institutions, noted in the first chapter, has given people a sense that things are out of control. No matter how hard we try we do not seem capable of ordering the impending chaos. We are trapped by it and our sin. Only God can re-create order. Thus it is a very meaningful image in our day to speak of God's struggle with the forces of chaos and evil in order to create new good.

The relevance of the classic view for today and its ability to affirm certain core biblical themes is undisputed. Questions may be raised about its ability to account adequately for the full scope of the biblical witness, particularly with reference to those texts which describe the atonement in terms of sacrifice or substitution. A fourth theory of the atonement, held most recently by contemporary theologians, Wolfhart Pannenberg and Regin Prenter, has implicitly sought to integrate the classic view with the satisfaction theory.

A fundamental commitment of this fourth view is that the law must be understood first, not as God's enemy, but as an expression of God's mercy. The law is good and perfect; it orders God's creation (cf. Ps. 19:7–8; 1 Tim. 1:8-9). Essentially these theologians regard the law in terms of natural law (the idea that the law is built into the structures of creation).[3]

The law is structured, however, in such a way that there exists a necessary connection between punishment and an evil deed. Thus our sin naturally brings punishment upon us. It is important at this point to recognize that the punishment of the law inflicted on sin is not something externally added by the wrath of God. The very structure of creation demands such punishment.[4] As such the law has become a kind of enemy to God's loving purpose. The only way to restore humanity to covenant fellowship is to conquer this law which is out of control. (The language here suggests the classic view's understanding of the law as God's enemy, which Christ overcomes in the atonement.) Yet the law in its original intention cannot be destroyed by Christ's conquest, for to destroy the law in that way would be to destroy creation, which is founded on the law. Thus Christ's conquest of the law's punishing function, which is out of control, must take the form of a substitutionary sacrifice, bearing the law's punishment on behalf of humanity.[5] For only in this way can the law be restored to its original intention. This language of sacrifice suggests the satisfaction theory. Thus in this fourth way of talking about the atonement we have a synthesis of the preceding two views.

The very fact that all four ways of describing the atonement appear in Scripture certifies the validity of each. Presumably Christians are justified in using all four in describing the atonement. As each view has particular strengths and weaknesses, each has been or could be best used in certain specific circumstances in the life of the church. (An identification of appropriate contexts for the use of these various ways of dealing with the atonement and other doctrines considered is a task for another day.) All share one very basic commitment. It is a necessary presupposition of all views that Jesus Christ can only be the agent of the atonement if he is both God and man. In the moral influence theory he cannot function to exemplify the life of faith unless he is truly human. In the classic view he cannot be truly engaged in overcoming the forces of evil unless he is fully immersed in the human condition. Likewise in the satisfaction theory and our fourth synthetic theory, it cannot be said Jesus has acted as humanity's substitute in bearing punishment for our sin unless Jesus is truly human. All four views correspondingly necessitate the affirmation that Jesus is God. If he were not, then it would follow that humanity, not God, is the agent of reconciliation. Only if Jesus is both God and human can the doctrine of justification by grace through faith and the biblical witness that it is God who saves (Jer. 30:10; 1 Sam. 14:39.) be affirmed. Atonement, incarnation, and the affirmation that we are redeemed by God's work are intimately connected, as is only proper.

One more consideration remains on this topic. We have considered what the atonement is. Now we must raise the question of what it accomplishes. The twentieth-century Reformed theologian, Karl Barth, has claimed that only two answers can be given to this question.[6] The atonement may be understood as creating a *possibility* for salvation. That is to say Christ's work is understood to create a situation whereby salvation can be offered to humanity, such that it will be theirs if they believe. In short, salvation is contingent upon faith. There are certainly biblical passages which suggest this (cf. Mark 16:16; 1 Cor. 15:2). However, by the same token, we have already noted that one also finds the New Testament witness referring to the universal thrust of God's grace (cf. Rom. 11:26; 2 Cor. 5:19; 1 Tim. 2:4; 1 John 2:2). Thus Barth concludes that we must offer a second answer to the question of what the atonement accomplishes. We may speak of the atonement's having created an *actuality* of salvation for all people, regardless of their response of faith.

This notion of actuality can be understood in several ways. It may imply an unambiguous affirmation of universal salvation (see chapters four and fourteen). In other cases, as for Barth himself, the possibility of an individual's rejection of the gift of the atonement is held in tension with the hope for universal salvation.[7] Further, it might be possible to correlate this view of the actuality of the atonement with the Reformation commitment to salvation through faith alone. Then it would follow that Christ's atoning work creates an actuality of salvation for all people, insofar as all are given the promise that they will come to faith. (1 Peter 3:19 and 4:6 suggest this idea that all might come to faith, even those who have not yet heard the gospel. It is claimed that Christ's descent into hell involved preaching the gospel to the dead that they might come to faith.) This understanding of what the atonement accomplishes, and a classic (or synthetic) view of the atonement is the perspective of this volume and the following sermon.

The sermon employs an imperfect human analogy in order to clarify the importance of the atonement for Christians' self-understanding and their understanding of God's love. A disturbing tendency in the contemporary church has been to focus on God's love to the neglect of the cross and resurrection. God's love is impoverished by such neglect of the atonement. The depth of God's love and its transforming power are nowhere more clearly evident than in the cross of Christ and his empty tomb.

§

Text: Hebrews 10:11–18
(*Preached in blue-collar congregation.*)

I still remember fondly my old 1970 Hornet. It was my first car, my first *real* car. It was a white, stripped-down model, as basic a car as only American Motors could make in those years. It was not much of a car by ordinary standards, but to me it was great. Great, because I earned most of the money to buy it (my parents helped some) prior to my senior year in college. As the years went by my Hornet became even more precious. Although my love for it in no way approximates God's love, my feeling still says something to me about how God's love for ordinary human creatures was enhanced by the experience God had gone through with them (see Isa. 43:1–4).

That 1970 Hornet was and is certainly a car of beautiful and warm memories. It was the car I had when I graduated from college and went off to begin my stay at Yale. It was the car I had when my wife, Betsey, and I met. We used that car on our first and most of our succeeding dates. We left on our wedding day in that car; the old white Hornet was our honeymoon vehicle. We started life together with it, visited families with it, moved with it. Then came that fateful day of decision in 1979, when it looked as though we would have to sell the old car for junk. I can still feel the tension. It helps focus for me more clearly the significance of Jesus' passion and the meaning of his victory over sin and death.

Understanding the reason for Christ's death has always been a problem for Christians. The early church struggled with this question. Today in our more permissive, narcissistic society we have an equally difficult time with the idea that Jesus' death atones for our sin. We like to think of God as love, love so great that it forgives all our sin (1 John 4:16–17). That is fine up to a point. Yet because in our society we tend to equate forgiving love with permissiveness, the next step is to think of ourselves as forgiven simply by God's permissive indulgence without reference to God's work. Because God is love, the slate is wiped clean; God overlooks our sin. Love understood in terms of permissiveness implies that sin is not really all that bad. There is no price to pay for evil in a permissive society with its permissive god.

Be honest, friends: am I not hitting home? In those moments when we get away from our legalistic tendencies (thinking we have to earn God's love) are we not likely to focus our thoughts and prayers on the soothing idea of God's love rather than on Christ and his disturbing cross? I know I have to plead guilty. At least I tended to ignore the cross until that day when our neighborhood garageman, Al, pronounced a death sentence on my precious old Hornet.

The old car was on its last legs. I had had it almost ten years, and it was well over the one-hundred-thousand-mile mark. We had taken many trips to the garage with it in recent years. In fact money was going down the tubes so quickly that Betsey and I began to think it would be cheaper to buy a new car or just get rid of the Hornet altogether, but I just couldn't let it go. We had been through too much together. My feelings for my car remind me of a love song God once sang to Israel through the prophet Isaiah. They had been through so much together: creation, escape from Egypt, flight to the promised land. And even though they sinned, God could not let them go. ". . . you are precious in my eyes," he said, "and honored, and I love you" (Isa. 43:1–4a). No, I could not let my old car go, even though our mechanic said it was hopeless. The car simply could not be repaired; it would have to be rebuilt and a new engine installed. In much the same way God could not let us go, even though our sin had made us hopeless. We would require rebuilding; God would need to give us a new heart (cf. Eph. 4:18–24). Strangely enough, there are perhaps some parallels, after all, between Christ's atoning work and my efforts to save our precious old car.

Back to the Hornet—Al advised us to sell it for junk. The engine block was cracked. The car could only run again if the existing engine were taken out and a new one put in. That would be very expensive, costing more than the car was really worth. And even if the new engine were put in, there would be no promises. What could we do? We grieved, just as God grieves over us and our sin (Gen. 6:6).

Betsey and I talked about it. We just could not bear to give up on the car that quickly. We agonized over whether to risk wasting our money (which was scarce) in a sentimental rescue effort. All the possibilities were weighed again and again.

Finally we took the risk and brought the car to Al's garage. What a day that was! I drove the car the five miles from our house to the garage and gave the keys to Al, but somehow I simply could not go home. It would have been easier, but I could not leave. I had to get involved. Little as I know about cars, I was out in the repair area participating in the action, fetching equipment for Al as he needed it. I find no satisfaction in mechanical endeavors! But I pitched in as best I could. There was too much riding on the repair of that car. My full participation in Al's efforts came from the love I felt for it.

In much the same way God could not leave us (cf. Ps. 37:33; 1 Kings 8:57). God had to get involved. John tells: "By this we know love, that he laid down his life for us" (1 John 3:16). My experience trying to save my car that day in Al's garage gave me some good handles on the significance Christ's atoning work has for us today. Although it would have been easier for me to stay at home or buy a new car, I could not because I loved that one too much. Likewise though, perhaps God might have found other means of making us new and forgiving our sins. Love for us required a total investment in the repair process. Just as we risked our precious dollars in the repair of our car, so God risked the infinitely more precious only Son. This is what happened when Jesus took up his cross.

If we forget Christ's atoning work on the cross and just focus on God's love, then we compromise the radicality of that love. It would be as if I told you I loved my old white car but had sold it for junk the minute Al said the word. My involvement in and agony over its repair testifies to my affection. That is in part what Christ's atoning work on the cross is about. God's love for us is affirmed all the more by personal participation in our repair/resurrection. The significance of Christ's atoning work for us today lies right here. The atonement conveys the costliness of God's love for you and me in the deepest and most intense way. Christ's death on the cross is really good news!

However Christ's death on the cross is not the last word. The resurrection must also be considered. Likewise, back to my old white car.

I stayed in Al's garage that day because I loved that car. Emotionally and financially I had a lot riding on its rebirth. Jesus had much more riding on our rebirth, so he hung on the cross because he loved us. Yet there is more to the atonement than merely acting out of God's love for us. Christ's work on the cross actually accomplished our salvation, made it happen. There was a resurrection of sorts in Al's garage that day in 1979. The old Hornet emerged running again. Yet it was not the same car; the old engine had died to make way for the new. Likewise in the cross we and our sinful natures have died through Christ to make way for the new creation.

We do not own the old car anymore. When we moved we realized we would not need a second car so we offered the Hornet to my parents who could use a second car at that time.

Today the Hornet has new owners and much better surroundings. It sleeps at night in a garage, which is something the old car never did in all its years with me. In short, its resurrection has provided it with a superior mode of existence. Thus it is with Christians as a result of Christ's atoning work. His death and resurrection have made for us a costly passageway into new life. Through him we have been given a radically new and better way of life. To talk about God's love apart from the atonement suggests that God has merely forgiven us our sins and that we are still the same old people we were before. We need to proclaim Christ's atoning work in order to appreciate the radical transformation God's love has brought about in us.

This analogy summarizes what the atonement can mean for us today. The next time you are tempted to talk or think about God's love for you without considering Christ's suffering, death and resurrection, remember my old car. Just as my love for that car brought about its transformation, so the atonement dramatically conveys the word that God's love for us can bring about our rebirth.

Who needs to focus on the atonement? We do. Christ's death and resurrection show us how intensely God loves us and how that love transforms and makes us new creatures. The atonement makes the good news of God's forgiving love even better! Amen.

Chapter Eight

JUSTIFICATION

The Pauline doctrine of justification by grace through faith apart from works of the law (Gal. 2:16; Rom. 3:24, 28) is the starting point for all Christian theological reflection. That is not to say it is the central or chief doctrine for all Christians, although several Reformation traditions make this claim.[1] Others like the Methodist, Baptist, Roman Catholic, and Orthodox traditions do not place so explicit an emphasis on it. Yet all Christians must begin with the doctrine in a very fundamental way. Justification by grace through faith asserts that salvation is totally the work of God. *Grace* refers to God's unmerited favor and love. Thus what humans do has no bearing on what God does for us by grace. As a result, if justification is by grace then salvation must be an action accomplished by God alone. (In this sense the doctrine of justification is closely correlated with the doctrine of election. See chapter four.) This means that all dimensions of the Christian life—piety, good works, and the like—must also be understood as works of God. All Christian communities agree on this matter. Disagreements arise merely over the role believers play in cooperating with God in these areas.

The Greek equivalent term for justification (δικαίωσις) literally means "a setting right." We could say it means to be "made righteous," but only with certain stipulations. There has been a tendency in both popular piety and formal theology to argue that to be made righteous in justification means that we are given the quality of righteousness. Thus justification entails an essential change in the believer.

Paul, by contrast, understands the "righteousness of God" (δικαιωσύνη θεοῦ) not as a quality or characteristic in God given to the believer, but rather as a term which refers to God's fulfillment of the promises to the patriarchs. This is evident insofar as Paul argues that the righteousness of God is revealed through faith in Jesus Christ and the work of redemption (Rom. 3:21-26). For Paul, Christ is the end of the law (Rom. 10:4), the offspring to whom the promises of the covenant were made (Gal. 3:16). Christ undertook his task in order to "confirm the promises given to the Patriarchs" (Rom. 15:8). This implies that the righteousness of God is revealed in the work of Christ in fulfillment of these promises. Therefore the term "righteousness of God" is truthfulness to and fulfillment of promises to the patriarchs. It is not some moral quality in God. Thus to say that we are made righteous in justification seems not to include on Pauline grounds any reference to an essential change in the believer's moral state. It is simply to say that believers have received the fulfillment of God's promises to Abraham.

This brief word study of the concept "righteousness of God" lends itself nicely to Lutheran and Reformed understandings of justification to the extent that both insist that justification brings about no essential change in the believer. In these traditions justification is in no way related to human cooperation or moral rectitude.[2] The word study has relevance for all segments of the church insofar as the preceding conclusion provides biblical evidence which supports the catholic belief that justification is God's work by grace alone.

Ecumenical agreement that justification is by grace apart from works of the law was achieved at the Council of Ephesus in A.D. 431, which climaxed the Pelagian controversy. We have noted the issues previously in the chapter on sin. Pelagius taught that human beings still have a will free to choose between sin and perfection. Grace was helpful but not necessary for living the Christian life. The leading spokesman for the orthodox position was the great North African Bishop St. Augustine. Augustine, who inspired the sixteenth-century Reformers, insisted that one cannot remain upright (be justified) apart from divine aid. In order to undergird this point he developed the doctrines of original sin and predestination. These underlined humanity's complete dependence on the grace of God. Ephesus essentially agreed with Augustine, not only on biblical grounds, but also because Pelagianism seemed to undercut the necessity of baptism. (The council did not endorse Augustine's notion of predestination. As noted in chapter four this issue continues to be debated hotly in Christian theology.) The biggest problem of Pelagianism was that it undercut the glory of God by making it possible for humans to live quite nicely without God. If we can justify ourselves by our works we do not let God be God, for we attribute to ourselves a work that belongs to God alone. All segments of Christendom are united in rejecting these Pelagian implications and in affirming that justification is by grace alone.

Pelagianism still remains a problem for the contemporary church. One can often discern its tendencies in popular piety. There is something about human nature which leads it to usurp God's glory and take the credit for itself. To live life as if one's well-being and salvation were totally or in part contingent upon one's performance is to rob God of glory, to take on tasks which belong to God. To live life on these terms is to be under a burden which is too heavy to bear. It can only lead to undue pride and eventually to despair when we realize we cannot fulfill the demands of providing for ourselves. The message of justification by grace sets us free from these burdens. As we noted in the first chapter it speaks an important word to our contemporary situation. In a society filled with persons seeking to find or make themselves, justification by grace means that God has done this for us. The church needs always to be on guard to keep this doctrine uncontaminated by our "innate" Pelagian tendencies.

As already noted, consensus among Christians on this doctrine breaks down over questions of its centrality, the role assigned to human cooperation, and justification's effect on the believer. At least four different treatments of the doctrine of justification may be identified.

The most venerable approach is the Eastern Orthodox Church's notion of *theosis/deification*. This is the idea that the incarnation,

God becoming human, has transformed human nature. The incarnation has provided human nature with a divine principle so that it is possible for humans to elevate themselves to a divine status. "God became man so that man might become like God."[3]

In some sense it is improper to identify this notion of theosis with justification. The Eastern Orthodox Church does not operate with such a concept. What in effect happens is that justification and sanctification (personal holiness) are virtually identified, the concern being to show that grace has indeed made a change in the human situation. Justification has resulted in an essential change in human nature. This implies a necessary role for human cooperation with grace in bringing about justification. Humans cooperate in helping to realize their godlikeness given by Christ.

A second approach to justification, the Roman Catholic-Scholastic position, bears great affinities to the Eastern Church's view. Although the claim is not made that grace renders us godlike, traditional Catholicism has regarded grace as an internal quality infused into human beings. It brings about an internal change in the believer. Believers are responsible for cooperating with this infused grace in order to complete the process of justification. Justification is a process insofar as it includes several logically distinct steps: (1) infusion of grace, (2) movement of the human will towards God, (3) movement of the will away from sin (repentance), and (4) remission of sins. This last step implies that justification is not complete until we are totally sanctified/holy.[4]

The advantage of both of these first views of justification is that they take seriously the transforming power of grace and the importance of human responsibility for living the Christian life. These views are clearly not Pelagian. The human role in justification is always understood as inspired by grace.

Questions may be raised about the biblical adequacy of these views in light of the word study of Paul's concept of righteousness at the outset of this chapter. The study's conclusions raise questions about the claim of these views that justification brings about an internal and essential change in the believer. Of course, one can identify passages in the New Testament which refer to godly characteristics (κατά θεόν: 2 Cor. 7:9) and the role of human initiative in striving towards salvation (cf. Phil. 3:13–14). These references lend some support to these views of justification. The Bible may be rich enough to support a plethora of alternatives. Historically the argument raised against the Eastern and Catholic view (at least during the Reformation) was related, not just to their improper biblical foundation, but also to their Pelagian tendencies.

It is true that the first two views of justification considered are in no way Pelagian. However, the insistence on the role of human cooperation with grace in justification more easily lends itself to Pelagian distortions than the next two approaches to justification which will be considered. This tendency was evident in the period immediately prior to the Reformation. Certain Roman Catholic theologians held that the human will might act independently of infused grace. In so doing the believer merited grace for subsequent justification. This view, since repudiated by Catholicism, led to the Reformation. It was deemed unbiblical and Pelagian by Reformers like Luther and Calvin.

It is a tragedy that a misrepresentation of one of these views of justification should have led to the church's schism. In fact, the Roman Catholic and Orthodox positions do not significantly diverge from Protestant positions insofar as they all affirm Paul's commitment to justification by grace, apart from works of the law. The schism is all the more tragic inasmuch as the Roman Catholic notion of the role of the will in justification has been accepted by some segments of Protestantism.[5] Also the Orthodox view bears some affinities to the fourth view of justification which I shall soon present.

The Pelagian tendencies of the views thus far considered have important practical implications for the life of faith. There is a great danger that the comfort and security of justification by grace through faith may be compromised by an insistence on the cooperating role of the human will. Even though it is understood that the believer's role in justification is always inspired by grace, the question can arise as to whether I have done enough. If not, I am not justified. I may not be acceptable to God just as I am. Because these views can compromise the security and certainty of faith they need to be supplemented or replaced by one of the next two approaches.

The third approach to this doctrine is called *forensic justification*. It is the polar opposite of the first two approaches. It is aimed at extolling the grace of God apart from any hint of human cooperation. In this view justification is understood according to a legal metaphor. We are justified in the sense that we are declared (ἔνδειξις) righteous. It is as if we were brought into a court of law, guilty of some offense, yet the judge declares us not guilty. Thus although we are guilty in fact, we are not guilty in the eyes of the court. So it is with Christians. They are simultaneously guilty and not guilty, saints and sinners (*simul iustus et peccator*).

The existential strength of this approach to justification is that it clearly attests to God's acceptance of believers exactly as they are without regard to any stipulations concerning their behavior or piety. There is great comfort in this. Also our complete dependence on grace is unambiguously affirmed. The question which may be raised with this approach is how grace makes a difference in the believer's life. The danger is the development of the attitude that grace is cheap. (We can do whatever we want because we are justified anyway and we are just as miserable sinners as we were before.) Or one could turn to the law as a way of prodding believers to live the Christian life. (This has often been the case in Reformation traditions.)

Some of these possible abuses are addressed by the fourth model for justification. We may call this model *justification as union with (conformity to) Christ*. This was the approach employed in the first chapter. It provides the viewpoint of the following sermons. This approach shares forensic justification's commitment to speaking of justification apart from any reference to human cooperation. Yet it is also concerned to indicate the impact justification has had on the believer. This is done by asserting that in justification the believer is joined to Christ in so intimate a union that what belongs to Christ is given to the believer. Christ's life and his conquest of death become mine. Justification provides the believer with an entirely new identity. (See chapter one.)

Although there are some points of convergence with the Eastern Church's view of theosis, this approach to justification differs from theosis in that no essential change in the believer is posited. The believer does not become godlike. Rather, believers are transformed, made Christlike, in the sense that one is transformed through any intimate relationship, such as with one's spouse. One becomes Christlike in justification in the sense that after years of marriage partners begin to think and act alike. Given this view, good works follow spontaneously from justification. They need not be an object of special attention. Works follow spontaneously from faith in the sense that spouses who love each other enjoy serving each other and meeting each other's needs. This is essentially one of the approaches to justification taken by Luther, Calvin, and other Protestants.[6] There is a place within these suppositions for paying attention to the lifestyle of a Christian. Yet one gets at this matter, not by urging Christians to do good works but simply by describing what justification through Christ has done to them. Baptism and justification transform Christians in the sense that a new identity is given to them.

The following sermon provides further illustration of this approach to justification, of how good works follow from justification. It also speaks to the profound existential meaning of the doctrine for our everyday lives. (It should be noted that references to our "coming to God" in faith presuppose that these phenomena are God's work. Chapter ten on the Holy Spirit will clarify this.) The church needs to affirm justification in all circumstances and do a better job proclaiming it than it has done. To know that we are justified, accepted, and affirmed is an insight and a reality which gives us confidence for facing both life and death. To know that the one who created life affirms me is to make living a joy.

§

Text: Romans 5:6–11
(*Preached in suburban congregation.*)

Today is a great day for a Lutheran Christian to be preaching. Why? Because today's second lesson, Romans 5:6–11, is all about the doctrine of justification through faith alone, the idea that sparked Martin Luther and started the Reformation. This is Christianity's chief and central doctrine, and today's second lesson gets right down to it. Paul tells us that we are justified through faith alone and not by what we do. He goes on to say that while we were God's *enemies*, even then, God loved us and became friends with us.

Justification through faith alone: for Christians of the Reformation tradition this is what Christianity is all about. This is the real meat of it. Perhaps you never heard the exact words before, yet my guess is that your pastor has been telling you a lot about it from this pulpit over the years. It is really the good news of God's love for you. Have you ever heard that before? Then you know what justification is. It is true: God loves you, people; God loves you. What that means is that we are justified, we have been made God's friends and have become heirs to all God's promises, not because of what *we* have done, but rather because God loved us while we were still God's enemies. We have not done anything to earn it. Yet Jesus died for us when we were helpless and undeserving.

All this has been accomplished by God. We have only to say yes to it. That is what faith is: saying yes, grabbing hold of and trusting in what God has done. Thus we are justified, saved, not by what we do, but by what God does for us. You and I do not *earn* God's love through playing a "brownie point" game. God loves us just the way we are.

God wants to have a love affair with you and me. God is courting us. Believe it or not, God has been courting us all our days. The courtship began when God made the covenant promises to the people of Israel in the Old Testament. Just like any lover, God deserves an answer. That answer is faith. This is why we speak of justification through faith alone. The promises of God have their fullest impact on us through our saying yes to them in faith.

The doctrine of justification boils down to the good news that God is inviting us to a love affair. That is what Christianity is all about. God is in love with us; God's love created us. Like all lovers, God has found a lot in us which is likeable. Even when we were enemies God loved us and found something about us to be lovable. God likes us just the way we are.

Talking about the doctrine of justification in this way makes me think of the theological research I am currently doing. I have been studying and writing about one of the great Christian theologians of our time, a Swedish scholar named Gustaf Aulén. This week I read something written recently by Aulén. That is exciting because Aulén is in his nineties. At any rate he was talking in the book about the very thing we are talking about today, the meaning of justification through faith and the good news of Jesus. He said, "The watchword of the gospel is: 'Come as you are.' "[7]

Come as you are. Think about this. It is great, isn't it? That is what Christianity is all about. Come as you are. I know it really speaks to me. That is the heart of our faith. God calls us to come just as we are.

This is the way love works, is it not? You can come as you are. "I don't care if you think you will be a drag, not up to your best. I do not care; I just like being with you. So just come; come as you are." There is a genuine security, a beautiful peace tied to this insight. To make a somewhat frivolous comparison, I receive a real boost because I know that my wife will still accept me even if the next time we go out my hair is not combed. (It usually is not.) Likewise I sense the same security in knowing that she will still love me even if I act as though I were out in space because I am thinking about something else. It is a real boost, it makes being Mark Ellingsen pretty great, to know that she is still there saying, "It is okay, Mark; come as you are. I love you anyway."

I have been excited this week about the insight that God, too, wants us to come as we are. In this light the remarks in today's assigned lessons make even more sense. In the lesson from Romans, the one we have been talking about, we hear that even when we were helpless enemies of God, God loved us and made friends with us. People, come as you are.

Also consider the Gospel Lesson (Matt. 9:35—10:7). Jesus saw crowds of people and had pity on them because of their diseases and tragic life. He sent his disciples out to tell them the good news of God. "People," he seemed to say, "come as you are."

The same word is even found in the first lesson (Exod. 19:2–6). Out in the desert, some thirteen-hundred years before the birth of Christ, a ragtag assembly of nomads was gathered together. They had only recently escaped from slavery in the land of Egypt. They were indeed a sorry-looking bunch. Yet God said to them, "People of Israel, you shall be 'a kingdom of priests and a holy nation'" (Exod. 19:6). People of Israel: come as you are.

The theme of justification by grace through faith appears in all the lessons. It certainly is great to be loved like that. God has a great love affair going with us. However, the Scripture lessons also show us that something else happened to the people of Israel after God's love came to them. They truly became that kingdom of priests, just as God had said.

I am sure you have learned that for us Lutherans and other Protestants not just the church's worship leaders are considered to be priests. On the contrary, we are *all* priests (1 Peter 2:9). We are all called to live our lives in the service of God. This is what happened to the people of Israel. That ragtag assembly of desert nomads, despite their ups and downs, kept the worship of God alive. God's love for them made a difference in who they were.

Consider the Gospel lesson (Matt. 9:35—10:7). It talks about twelve ordinary people like you and me, people who had heard Jesus say: "Come as you are." It made a difference in their lives. They left their jobs and families, followed Jesus, and even got themselves ready to go out and tell everybody the good news. Those twelve ordinary men were never quite the same after they met Jesus.

That is not very surprising, is it? Is that not the way love works? It changes you. I am not the same person I was when my wife and I fell in love. At least I hope I am not. I am not quite the same person as that twenty-year-old college student who was sure there was no God until a wise professor stuck a book by Martin Luther in his hands. I am not the same. At least I hope I am not.

That is the way love works. If you are really involved, it changes you. God's love has an effect on us just like it had on Jesus' twelve ordinary men and on the people of Israel. They came to God as they were, but they were not quite the same after experiencing God's love.

I am really tempted to return to Aulén's words of wisdom and add an amendment to them. The message of Jesus is really twofold. Come as you are; you will not leave the same way. You will be a different person than you were before. You will have a new identity.

Love changes people. You do not leave the same way you came. Yet a love relationship does not begin until you know that you are totally accepted by the other person. That is what Christianity (the doctrine of justification by grace through faith) is all about: you can come to God as you are. However, when you do come it will make a difference. You cannot share close relationships with other people without being transformed by them, without sharing in their good qualities. It is that way in our relationship with God. It makes us new people.

God says to the people of this congregation: come as you are! There is great peace and security in that statement. It is a wonderful feeling to know that you are affirmed at the very core of your being by the one who created life. Come as you are, and you will not leave the same way you came. You have a new identity that works to make your life and this whole parish shout with joy about how good God's love really is. This is the gospel of the doctrine of justification by grace through faith. Come as you are. You will not leave the same way you came. Amen.

Chapter Nine
SANCTIFICATION AND THE CHRISTIAN LIFE

Sanctification (ἁγιασμός) literally means to be "made holy," "set apart." Believers are made holy and set apart as a consequence of justification insofar as they are brought into union with Christ and his body, the church. To belong to the body is to be called out or set apart from the world. (This happens in baptism.) Thus justification implies "set apartness." To be set apart with some religious end in view is by definition to be holy. That is the status of the justified. They are holy people, called out from the world by virtue of belonging to Christ's body. As such they are not morally holy, but holy in the sight of God. In this sense, to the degree justification is understood as a completed event and not a process, Christians are made completely holy in justification and baptism.

Sanctification also refers to the Christian life. This is perhaps our greatest interest in the topic. The root word for the Greek term (ον ἅγιος) reveals this. This root means "consecrated for service to God." In this sense sanctification is not complete, but rather in process. Service to God never ends for the Christian; therefore, sanctification is not complete. In this life the Christian never serves God fully and perfectly. Sin always leads us to serve other masters as well. Thus we are not completely sanctified for we do not serve God with all our heart, soul, and mind. In this respect sanctification is a process. Justification starts us on a life of service to God.

To summarize, the doctrine of sanctification refers to two

realities. First it refers to the believer's holiness (set-apartness) in the sight of God (*coram deo*). In this sense, to the degree justification is a completed event, sanctification is also complete. The doctrine's second referent is the Christian's service to God. In this sense sanctification is not complete; it is an ongoing process. This leads us to a consideration of three questions with which we must deal in this chapter: (1) what is the content of sanctification and the Christian life and what sort of a lifestyle does it entail? (2) what are the implications of the doctrine of sanctification for the Christian's involvement in the institutions and structures of society? and (3) what is the relationship between sanctification and justification?

The first question will not be dealt with in much detail at this point. The content of the Christian life is identical with baptism (and union with Christ). We will say more about this in chapter twelve when we discuss baptism. Essentially the Christian life given in baptism is characterized by a death-resurrection motif. By being united with Christ, we die to sin as he died. Yet the little deaths we die (the times we deny ourselves) are passageways to life, as his death was the passageway to resurrection (Rom. 6:1–11). Related to this insight is a point we raised in the first chapter and have pursued throughout this presentation of Christian doctrine. The identity given Christians in their faith and baptism entails participation with Christ in God's ongoing process of creating new good. To be a Christian, then, is to be a creative person who seeks to bring good out of every situation in life. This act of creating good is done by denying the self for the good of the neighbor in self-emptying love (*agape*). All characteristics and qualities which Scripture attributes to believers should be understood in light of this framework. They are either descriptions of the Christian's self-sacrificing love or they reflect the Christian's creative identity. In the sense that sanctification is complete, these qualities describe the Christian's new identity given in justification. Insofar as sanctification is regarded as a process, they are characteristics which the Christian is coming to approximate.

This discussion of the content of sanctification and the Christian life leads us to their implications for the Christian's involvement in societal structures. The topic of Christian social ethics really deserves a chapter in itself. Nevertheless, we can begin with some reflections. Initially we should note that the holiness given or nurtured in sanctification is not a personal holiness. That is, it is not a personal characteristic in which the believer can revel apart from service to the neighbor. Christians cannot be holy in isolation from others or apart from the body of Christ. The question then becomes who is the neighbor I am to serve.

H. Richard Niebuhr's classic book, *Christ and Culture*, is the best resource for dealing with this question. Niebuhr identifies four classic responses to the issue of how Christians relate to the broader culture. I believe these four responses can be reduced to three. The first response is that of the *sect*. These Christians believe that holiness can only be nurtured in isolation from secular society, which is inherently evil. The neighbor to be served is the fellow believer who belongs to the sect. There is no attention paid to reforming (or even criticizing) the structures of soceity.

One cannot hold this view and still affirm the ongoing character of creation or its implication that Christ's redeeming work is an instance of God's ongoing creativity. A commitment to the ongoing character of creation and its implication has been the theological position of this volume. On these grounds, since redemption is an instance of creation and because creation has a universal thrust directed to all, it follows that those who are in Christ must share the same universal concern reflected in creation. This position renders the sect mentality impossible. Christians who share this nonsectarian position will inevitably understand their Christian responsibility in universal terms and so will be led to work for reform within the structures of society.

For these Christians, basically two different approaches to interacting with societal structures have evolved. The first should be called the *theocratic model*. In a theocracy the church either rules the state or the gospel has a direct impact on its affairs. The argument is that the state is ordained by God and its rulers are God's representatives. As such, those who represent God can only do so by using government to serve gospel's ends. There is certainly biblical support in the Old Testament to support this view. Even in societies where the gospel is not built into the legislative structure, the Christian's best contribution to society as a citizen is to call it back to the principles of the gospel. Only when the laws of the government are in harmony with the gospel can the state execute the function God has ordained for it.

The second approach to the Christian's interaction with society has been called the *two-kingdom ethic*. This view takes very seriously the Pauline injunction in Romans 13 which suggests that the state has its own integrity apart from the church. This is not to say that God has not ordained secular government. (This insight tended to be overlooked by certain German Lutherans during the Nazi era when the integrity of the state under the two-kingdom ethic was used to justify nonresistance to Nazi atrocities.) God has established the state as part of the created order. As we noted in the fourth chapter, creation is structured according to the principles of the law (Ten Commandments). Therefore those institutions built into the created order must have the law as their operating principle. Secular government is one of these institutions and so it must operate according to principles of the law. The task of the Christian, then, is to ensure that government is ruled by the principles of the second table (final six commands) of the Ten Commandments. That is to say, Christian responsibility entails that Christians work to see that the state truly serve God's ordained purpose for it by administering justice. Where the government is unjust, the Christian's duty is to work to see that justice is served. Christians are equally concerned about government with this approach as with the theocratic model. The difference is that their endeavors at sharing in the creation of new goods in society are done according to the guidance of the law, not the gospel. To do otherwise, to attempt to inject the gospel into the dynamics of government, is to confuse the gospel with the law. When that happens the doctrine of justification by grace through faith apart from works of the law may be compromised. The gospel may be heard as law since in the sphere of social ethics it is being legislated as though it were law. Protecting the integrity of the gospel and the doctrine of justification, while still asserting the Christian's responsibility for secular society, is the rationale for the two-kingdom ethic approach.

This discussion of the shape of the Christian life brings us to a consideration of our final question on this topic, the issue of motivation. Why should persons live the Christian life if they are already justified apart from works of the law? What is the relationship between justification and sanctification? Historically, Christians have answered these questions in a variety of ways.

The Eastern Orthodox and traditional Roman Catholic approaches to the problem of justification answer the question of motivation for good works quite directly. As we noted in the preceding chapter, some degree of Christian response to grace (sanctification) is a necessary precondition for justification. Issues related to sanctification quite naturally receive a great deal of attention in these traditions. We also noted in the preceding chapter the potential abuses of these approaches. They can compromise the security and certainty of justification because always lurking in the background is the anxiety that I may not be fulfilling my Christian responsibility well enough. If I fail, I am not justified.

For this reason the approach reflected in this volume has presented a different relationship between justification and sanctification. Rather than envisioning justification as contingent upon sanctification, I have followed the sixteenth-century Reformers who held that sanctification is a consequence of justification, that good works flow spontaneously from justification as we are conformed to and have union with Christ. In being conformed to him we become people who want to be "little Christs."(Rom. 6:2, 14; 8:5, 10–11 seem to support this view.)

Some Christians of the Reformation traditions holding this viewpoint have been uncomfortable with its systematic implications. It would seem that Christians would have no motivation for good works, for keeping the law. Can we really assume that Christians will in fact do the good just because they have been given a new identity in justification? Do we not need to provide additional motivation for Christians to do good works?

The Calvinist perspective is to regard perseverance and good works as signs of election.[1] Those who do good works can be assured that they are elect. Thus one motivation for doing good works is the assurance it brings individuals that they are among the elect (cf.

Phil. 1:6). An alternative to this mode of stimulating good works is found in Methodism and other pietist traditions. They argue that perfection in love should be set as a goal toward which the Christian may strive (see Phil. 3:12)[2]

Both of these modes of providing additional motivation for good works have been rejected by certain segments of the church. The concern may be, particularly from a Lutheran perspective, that an emphasis on Christian perfection as a goal could undercut an appreciation of the Christian as *simul iustus et peccator* (simultaneously saint and sinner). Even the redeemed creature is still sinner (Rom. 7:14ff.), and as such all our deeds are still tinged with sin. Even works of love are *brave-pious sins*.

At stake in these commitments is the endeavor to defend the centrality of justification by grace. The concern is that if Christians think segments of their lives are untouched by sin, they may not feel as much need to rely on Christ's redeeming work as the starting point and foundation of their lives. This commitment to asserting the centrality of justification leads those who hold this view to insist that no additional motivation for good works need be added to an awareness that good works follow spontaneously from justification. Justification by grace through faith alone is all that needs to be said on the topic. The supposition is, as we have seen in this volume, that justification and baptism provide believers with a new identity which wants to do good works and keep the law. The sermon in the preceding chapter (and that in the first chapter) particularly illustrates this approach.

Nevertheless, the question may still remain about what status good works have in Christian life. What should we make of them and the biblical directives and exhortations to Christian living (e.g., the book of James)? The following sermon, while still maintaining this volume's overall commitment to the fact that good works follow spontaneously from faith, tries to deal with these questions. The argument presupposes the peace and comfort of knowing that we are accepted by God "as we are." This good news and sense of acceptance transforms life into a joyous partnership with God in creating new good. Of course our creative projects are not ultimately important since God can get along without us. Thus the pressure for us to achieve these high goals is removed, and the Christian life becomes a wonderful kind of "game." We may experience the fun of realizing our identity in creative projects without fear of failure. One way, then, of understanding the doctrine of sanctification is to say that Christians do good works because they are a part of the joyful game which has been created by God's redeeming love. Just as every game has certain rules which are kept because they are good for the game, so Christians are given the law to help in living the Christian life. The difference of course is that the law is kept because of gratitude to God and because fulfilling the law's demands is part of our new identity (that in us which is no longer the same since coming to God as we are).

§

Text: Matthew 5:20–36

(*Preached in seminary chapel service.*).

> "For I tell you, unless your righteousness exceeds that of the scribes and Pharisees, you will never enter the kingdom of heaven. . . . But I say to you that every one who is angry with his brother shall be liable to judgment; whoever insults his brother shall be liable to the council, and whoever says 'You fool!' shall be liable to the hell of fire." (Matthew 5:20, 22)

These are hard words, are they not? What do you make of them? What is the Word of God for us in this text? It is obvious, is it not? At least it was obvious to several forebearers of our Reformation tradition. In the Sermon on the Mount (from which this text is taken) the law is proclaimed in such a way that it condemns sin.[3]

This sounds like a reasonable approach. At least it has always seemed correct to me. Yet I have been studying Matthew again lately, and I think there is more to the Sermon on the Mount than merely the condemnation of our sin. Much of what I have read indicates that these texts tell us something about the positive role of the law in the life of a Christian.[4]

The positive role of the law is a difficult question for many contemporary believers. We become a bit uncomfortable when we read that the champion of Christian freedom, Martin Luther, wrote that Christians may love the law and treat it like a god.[5] We do not want to hear it said that good works should be preached. We do not quite know how to deal with this. Freedom from the law is a much more comfortable topic in our permissive society. Yet Jesus' sermon gives us some clues to the positive function of law, the role of good works, in the life of a Christian.

In a passage immediately prior to the text we have been considering, Jesus says he has not come to abolish the law but to fulfil it (Matt. 5:17). That is more in harmony with the thinking of many of us who believe in the centrality of justification by grace through faith. Jesus has fulfilled the law for us; we are free from it. Toward the end of the sermon things even get better. Jesus is reported to have said: "Every one then who hears these words of mine and does them will be like a wise man who built his house upon the rock . . . and [the house] did not fall, because it had been founded on the rock" (Matt. 7:24). That is what we want to hear. We can do no good works apart from the rock who is Christ. Matthew is not such a bad Lutheran after all. Yet later in the sermon, when Jesus says that we should not worship God until we have cleared up the bad relationships we have with our neighbors, all of Matthew's good work seems to go down the drain. It is evident that Matthew thinks the law does have a positive significance for the Christian. Faith becoming active in love is even more important than worship. For him obedience to the law is an important ingredient in the life of a Christian.

Yet all this talk about obedience seems so absurd in view of the fact that at the outset of this text Jesus suggests that our own righteousness will never get us into the kingdom (Matt. 5:20). Jesus has fulfilled the law. Why, then, is keeping it so important that we should put it before worship? The law is obviously very important for Matthew; it plays a positive, not just a condemning, role for him. Yet works of the law do not justify. That is clear from what he has Jesus say. However, what are we to make of this positive significance of the law in our lives? Why should we Christians do good works? Why should we feel impelled to follow the directives of the Sermon on the Mount, inasmuch as the good news of justification by grace has set us free? I have an idea I want to try out on you. It is not a perfect analogy, but it may help us understand the relationship between grace and law. I propose that this text is implicitly saying that the role of good works and the law in a Christian's life is a little like the role table games and basketball play in my relationship with my friends Dave and Steve. They are good in themselves.

I have just returned from a wonderful Christmas vacation, and I think one of the best parts of it was seeing my old friends Dave and Steve. Dave and Steve are probably my two closest male friends. The older I get the more I realize what a special relationship we have. We talk about things and how we feel about each other the way textbooks about friendship and human relationship say you should. We have known each other a number of years. Steve was my college roommate, and Dave and I began our friendship in grade school.

My wife and I were driving East just as Christmas vacation began, and we started talking about Dave and Steve and their families. Betsey said, "You know when we get together it will not be long before we will all be playing Monopoly, and before the day is over you will probably play basketball." "No," I thought, "we have not seen each other for over a year." Yet as it turned out Betsey was right; playing table games and basketball is exactly what we did. I think that happened for the same reasons that Christians live in the law and do good works.

I should explain. It seems that whenever Dave, Steve, and I have gotten together over the years at some point we have wound up playing table games or basketball. With Dave and me this practice goes back to childhood. Now as adults the tradition continues. (The women we live with either like table games or they love us enough to put up with it.)

Yet all this is a bit odd. It is strange, because none of us are normally table game addicts. In fact I rarely play. I do not enjoy games much except with these friends; they seem to get better in the context of our relationship. In fact the relationship itself is what leads me to play them. In other situations I do not like those games and rebel against playing them. The law is a bit like that for Christians. In the context of our relationship with God it gets better. Apart from that context it brings about rebellion. However, in the context of a right relationship with God, the law is good in itself. In much the same way, table games and basketball are good in themselves for Dave, Steve, and me.

I have thought about our relationship. Why do we play those darn games? We do not do it to keep our friendship alive, because it is not founded on those activities. Dave and I may have met on a basketball court, but that was a long time ago. Games are not the foundation of my friendship with Steve. We knew each other for years before we ever played a table game. Our friendship is not grounded in those games. That is like the way the law functions for Christians. It is not the foundation for our relationship with God. Christ has fulfilled the law for us. Thus we keep the law and do good works because it is a good in itself, much like playing those games with Dave and Steve are fun, goods in themselves.

I should add more about our games in order to pursue this analogy. I do not always want to play them. I was not looking forward to it this time. Yet Dave said, "Come on, we gotta shoot hoops." I did not really want to play. Steve had left the day before. Yet playing ball was something Dave really wanted to do. So playing the game provided an occasion to love him, and I had fun doing it. The law works that way for Christians. It provides an occasion to love the neighbor. The law and good works, table games and basketball: in the context of a proper relationship they are rewarding and are fun in themselves.

You know it is a bit ludicrous. At least it would seem so to an outsider. After all, we are six adults, and none of us is quite as flighty as I have made it seem. Yet these six adults come together and play a silly children's game. At this table you will find a man who by choice is dedicating his life to teaching inner city minority children. Also present is a classic '60s rebel who is out to undercut the fraudulent claims of academic science. We are joined by three very capable and talented women, each successful in her own career. Finally this Lutheran clergyman joins the group. We are used to dealing with big, life and death issues, but together we play games. It is laughable; it gets us nowhere. It does not make or break our relationship. Yet we do it. It is a good fun thing in itself.

In the grand scheme of things that is the status of the law for

Christians. In its own way trying to keep the law is as ludicrous as the six of us playing games. It contributes nothing to our relationship with God. It gets us nowhere with God. It has no cosmic significance; God can get along without us. Yet Christians strive to keep the law and do good works, because like our table game it is good in itself. Just as I love playing those games with Dave and Steve, so Christians love the law. Christian life is a bit like playing a game.

What does playing table games have to do with keeping the law and loving our neighbor? Keeping this analogy in mind can help us sort things out. The trouble many of us have is that we make too much of the law, either by insisting that we have to do good works or by making the law a vicious enemy. In the latter case that becomes our excuse for never doing good works. We spend too much time worrying about an unimportant item. I propose to you that Christ has relegated the law to the status of a table game. The law is fulfilled. The problem is that we magnify our good works and the importance of Christian response. We are too concerned about avoiding cheap grace. In the ultimate scheme of things, keeping the law and doing good are like playing a table game. It gets you nowhere; it is absurd; it is ultimately inconsequential before God. Yet like our table game it is a good thing; it is fun to play and good for us and others.

Christian friends, the law of God commands you to make peace with each other even before you worship, to be honest and just in your relationships (Matt. 5:21–26). Why should we do these things since justification has set us free from bondage? We do these things because they are good in themselves. God has ordained it, but it is important always to remember that such deeds are about as significant ultimately as table games. Christ has fulfilled the law and set us free. Christ has transformed our keeping of the law into a kind of joyful game. That is real freedom. As Dave would put it, "Let's go and play." Like playing those games with my friends, living the Christian life is a joyful and exciting experience. Who would not want to play? Amen.

Chapter Ten
THE HOLY SPIRIT

The doctrine of the Holy Spirit has generally been neglected throughout most of the church's history. This is evident in the early church's failure to affirm the deity of the Holy Spirit. The earliest formal statement of Trinitarian doctrine at Nicea (A.D. 325) made scant reference to the Spirit except to affirm belief in the Spirit's existence. (Nothing very specific was stated in the original Nicene formula about the Spirit's relationship to the Godhead.) It was only when its relative neglect was recognized, as a consequence of the Montanist heresy, that the church began to give the doctrine of the Holy Spirit attention.

Montanism was a second-century apocalyptic movement whose adherents believed that the church must continue to anticipate Christ's imminent return and to refrain from structuring itself in more permanent forms designed to endure through time. In fact the church in the second century had begun to lose this apocalyptic vision. As a result, the extraordinary prophetic operations of the Spirit which had predominated in the New Testament church (see Acts 2:4ff.; 1 Cor. 12:7-10; 14:1-40; 2 Cor. 12:12; Gal. 3:5) were no longer occurring.

At this point in history, however, the church was unwilling to concede that the age of such extraordinary prophetic operations of the Spirit was over. This fact, coupled with a growing apocalyptic mentality nurtured by the persecution of Christians, makes it possible to understand the origins of Montanism. Precedent already existed in the early church for associating the Holy Spirit with eschatological expectations (having to do with the end times; see Joel 2:28-29; Acts 2:17-19). As the Spirit had been withdrawn from Israel after the exile so Montanists came to believe the Spirit had been withdrawn from the church because of its moral laxity. This observation, coupled with growing persecution, fostered a kind of apocalyptic sensibility which was ripe for belief in extraordinary manifestations of the Spirit. These movements of spiritual and prophetic ecstasy (e.g., speaking in tongues) in anticipation of Christ's imminent return characterized the Montanist movement.[1]

Montanism's greatest contribution to the development of the doctrine of the Holy Spirit, then, was that it called the early church's attention to the Spirit. The prophetic utterances made by the Montanists when caught up in spiritual ecstasy were no less influential. They tended to speak of the Holy Spirit in the first person. In doing so they typically related the Spirit to the other persons of the Trinity; they spoke in Trinitarian formulations. Thus the Montanists were important for calling the church to a more personal understanding of the Spirit.[2] That the Spirit could speak through individual adherents of the Montanist movement indicated that it could not merely be deemed a divine life-force or a divine activity. The Spirit must be deemed "personal" in the same way that Father and Son could be regarded as personal because they address humanity.

A second contribution made by Montanism to the development of the doctrine of the Holy Spirit is apparent in the ecstatic utterances of its adherents (and the influence of these utterances on liturgical forms), which tended to attribute divinity to the Spirit. These emphases created an impact on the early church's piety which rendered the original Nicene formulation inadequate. Their impact made it impossible for the fourth-century church to construe the Nicene formulation as a denial of the Spirit's divinity, despite the efforts of certain heretical groups like the *pneumatomachi* to do so. As such, Montanism indirectly fostered subsequent refinements of the Trinity doctrine.

Finally Montanism influenced the early church's theology in yet another way. In response to the Montanist insistence on continuing prophecy through ecstatic utterances worked by the Spirit, the church pushed the time of prophecy into the past. The period of revelation came to be regarded as having ended with the book of Revelation.[3] Henceforth the church would evaluate all contemporary prophetic utterances (preaching) by the authority of the biblical prophets. Thus Montanism indirectly contributed to the formalization of the authority of the biblical canon. As such it also suggested a principle of evaluating claims about the Spirit's work in relation to the written Word. As we shall see, this latter point is fundamental to a proper understanding of the Holy Spirit.

Despite these influences which would seem to have hastened the church's development of a doctrine of the Holy Spirit, the relatively late development of the doctrine is not difficult to understand. The biblical witness does not provide much clear, concrete information about the Holy Spirit. This lack of clarity, I think, accounts for the relative neglect of the doctrine throughout the church's history.

Since biblical times the church has been able to tell the Christian story, recount the mighty acts of God in creation and redemption, without reference to the Holy Spirit. This is evident in the propensity of several New Testament authors to speak in binitarian formulas, in terms of only Father and Son (cf. John 1:1-17; Col. 1:15-20). That the early church tended to avoid integrating the Holy Spirit in its telling of the Christian story is not surprising in view of the fact that the biblical witness provides no consistent pattern in its treatment of the Spirit. In fact one can identify four distinct, perhaps unrelated, ways in which the concept of "Spirit" appears in the Old and New Testament.

The Old Testament speaks of Spirit as breath of life or vitality (*ruach*). In some texts the *ruach* is a purely anthropological concept which refers to the common life-force. It equates with the term *nephesh* (cf. chapter four) which also refers to the life-force (cf. Gen. 6:17; 7:15; Ps. 31:5).

Of course Yahweh must also have *ruach*. It is God's creative force (Ps. 33:6; Gen. 1:2). It must be noted that these references to the Spirit of God do not unambiguously correlate with the New Testament notion of the Holy Spirit. For the New Testament regards the presence of the Holy Spirit as a sign of eschatological fulfilment. In order to appreciate this we must first proceed to note the subsequent development of the concept *ruach* in the Old Testament. For the present it is sufficient to note that both a tension and a mutual relationship have been created in the Old Testament witness—between a spirit that belongs to humanity and a spirit which is of God, between eternal Spirit of God and a Spirit associated with God's work in the end times.

Before the belief arose that God's Spirit would be manifest in working salvation on the day of Yahweh (the eschaton), a third understanding of the concept *ruach* developed. Prior to the exile (586 B.C.) the Israelites came to believe that Yahweh's Spirit manifested itself as extraordinary ecstatic power in certain individuals (charismatic leaders in war or prophets). This is evident in the gift of Yahweh's Spirit to Gideon (Judg. 6:34), Saul (1 Sam. 11:6), and David (1 Sam. 16:3).

It should be emphasized that unlike the New Testament understanding of the Holy Spirit, the gift of the Spirit in this period of the Old Testament was selective and temporary, not permanent and given to all. In fact in the period after the exile the Spirit no longer seemed to manifest itself. The prophets who did arise were given a kind of mandate by Yahweh, apart from any gift of the Spirit (see Isa. 8:11; Jer. 1:9). As a result, foundations were laid for a fourth stage in the development of the concept.

In this period when the Spirit was no longer manifest in Israel, the gift of the *ruach* came to be deemed for the first time an eschatological hope. Messianic prophecies identified the Messiah as the shoot of Jesse who would receive the Spirit permanently (Isa. 11:2). This correlation of Messiah and Spirit has proven to be a most important development for subsequent Christian theology. No less important is the later prophetic notion of the Spirit being poured out on all flesh (Ezek. 36:26-28; Joel 2:28). As these hopes failed, first-century Judaism came to deny totally the gift of the Spirit as a present reality, viewing it solely as an eschatological hope. The fourth step in the development of the concept of the spirit, the New Testament idea of the Holy Spirit as eschatological gift tied to the work of the Messiah had already been prefigured.

This analysis of the Old Testament understanding of *ruach* explains why it was necessary for the early church to come to terms with the Spirit in conjunction with Jesus' ministry. The reality of the Spirit was a necessary consideration for the church if it were to embrace its Jewish heritage. As already noted, certain understandings of the Spirit were already given by the Old Testament witness. However the diversity of this witness accounts for the difficulties the church has had in speaking of the Holy Spirit. The problem is how to integrate the four strands of the concept Spirit which we have noted: (1) the human spirit, (2) Yahweh's creative spirit, (3) the temporary gift of Yahweh's Spirit to Israel's leaders, and (4) the Spirit poured out on us as a sign of the end times. The difficulty in performing this task of integration accounts in part for the church's reticence in speaking of the Holy Spirit. To some degree subsequent developments in the doctrine of the Holy Spirit since the New Testament period can be understood as efforts to integrate these four biblical strands. The way in which these efforts were made was largely conditioned by the New Testament church's experience of the Holy Spirit. To a large extent this experience was consistent with the postexilic understanding of Spirit as eschatological gift.

There can be no doubt that the early church first experienced the Holy Spirit as a consequence of Jesus' ministry and his resurrection (John 14:16ff.; Luke 11:13; Acts 2:17ff.). As we have seen, this intimate connection between the Spirit and Christ and the idea that the Spirit would be poured out on all the faithful in eschatological fulfilment were already prefigured in the Old Testament (see 2 Cor. 1:22; Eph. 1:13-14). This intimate connection between Christ and the Spirit came to be the determining factor in subsequent development of the doctrine of the Holy Spirit (and so in integrating the various biblical strands we have identified).

The idea that the Spirit was revealed only in conjunction with Christ led New Testament writers like Paul to speak of the Holy Spirit as the Spirit of Christ (see Rom. 8:9; Gal. 4:6). This suggests that the Spirit should be regarded as nothing more than the ongoing and contemporaneous presence of Christ. The Spirit has no content other than Christ. The Spirit's task is nothing more than to make Christ present to us. In this way the Holy Spirit is highly relevant for contemporary believers. Because we know the Holy Spirit, we know that the historical distance between ourselves and Christ is being overcome, that he is *really* and *truly* among us. In this way the doctrine of the Holy Spirit is a great source of comfort and strength for our faith.

Several important implications for the doctrine of the Holy Spirit follow from these observations. First this intimate relationship between Christ and the Holy Spirit implies that the Spirit may reveal nothing which has not already been given by Christ (see John 16:13-15). The possibility of new revelations or prophecy is thereby undercut. We can see that the second-century church's rejection of Montanism and its idea of new prophecy not contained in the canonical Scriptures was legitimately grounded in the New Testament witness about the Holy Spirit.

A related implication is that if the Spirit only works in conjunction with Christ and reveals only what has been revealed in Christ, then it must follow that the Spirit only works through the means instituted by Christ. This is a very important point for understanding the work of the Holy Spirit. On this basis it follows that Christians believe that the Spirit only works through, or at least in agreement, with the means of grace—Word and sacrament. As was apparent in its response to Montanism, the church rejects all forms of *enthusiasm* (the claim to unmediated communion with God). Therefore Christians cannot claim that the Holy Spirit is acting simply because they have had some "spiritual" experience (e.g., speaking in tongues). Any claim that the Spirit is working among us must always be critically appraised in light of what we know about Christ and his work through Word and sacrament (see 1 John 4:1-3; 1 Cor. 13:1-3). The Christian doctrine of the Holy Spirit makes for a very common-sense approach to spiritual experiences. Christians need not affirm every mystical or occult experience they encounter as divine and authentic. Such experiences are works of God and not the human imagination only if they are in accord with what we know of Christ through Word and Sacrament.

The close correlation of the Holy Spirit and Christ entails yet one more important implication. It demands the divinity of the Holy Spirit, inasmuch as the Spirit's content is nothing other than the *divine* Christ. In effect it forces the church to integrate the second biblical strand pertaining to the concept "Spirit" (the idea of Yahweh's Spirit) with the eschatological concept of the Spirit.

The failure of the Nicene church to clarify the Holy Spirit's relation to God is not surprising in view of the tensions we have seen among the various strands in the biblical witness. However, a combination of the implications entailed by Scripture's close identification of the Spirit and Christ, the impact of the Montanist equation of the Spirit with God, and the bare liturgical fact that baptism must be in the name of the Holy Spirit (see Matt. 28:19) contributed to the necessity of the post-Nicene church's dealing with the question. On the basis of these factors and the fact that the Scripture attributed both divine titles and qualities to the Spirit (see Matt. 1:18; Rom. 1:4) and also attributed works to the Spirit that only God could do (like judging sin, see John 16:8-9, and making alive, see Rom. 8:11), the church was led to conclude that the Spirit must be divine. Like Christ, the Spirit must have the same *homoousios* (substance) as the Father.[4]

The problem for the late fourth- and fifth-century church was how to assert the divinity of the Holy Spirit and conceptualize the relationship between Spirit, Father, and Son. If the Spirit were divine then the Holy Spirit cannot have had a beginning and must be eternally with the Father. He must be identified with references to Yahweh's Spirit in the Old Testament. In working out the nature of this inter-Trinitarian relationship, the theologians of this era were very much dependent upon the presuppositions of the Council of Nicea. In fact, final refinements on the Trinity doctrine were carried out by theologians of this era while working out the question of asserting the Holy Spirit's divinity.

The problem faced by these theologians (the so-called Cappadocian Fathers: Basil, Gregory of Nazianzus, Gregory of Nyssa) was how to affirm the Nicene Creed's formulation that the Holy Spirit "proceeds from the Father." If the Spirit is eternal how can the Spirit proceed from the Father? If the Spirit is eternally with the Father what are we to make of Scripture's associating the Spirit with the end times and work of Christ? Several alternatives were foreclosed for these theologians because the Council of Nicea had condemned them. The Sabellian idea that the Holy Spirit was merely a mode or temporal activity of God had previously been repudiated. Further, the influence of Montanism necessitated that the Spirit be regarded as "personal" in some way.

As noted in our earlier discussion of the Trinity, the theologians of this period formulated the notion of one *ousia* and three *hypostases* as a way of dealing with this problem. This formula has received general recognition by the church as a way of conceptualizing the inter-Trinitarian relationships. Yet as we noted, no formal definition of these terms has ever been achieved. As a result, the questions raised in the preceding paragraph in regard to how we may account for the Spirit as eschatological gift while affirming that the Spirit has also been eternally with the Father remain unanswered. All that can be said with ecumenical certainty is that the Spirit is distinct from the Father in a personal way, yet shares the divine being and so shares in the divine activities. Insofar as the church has not provided authoritative doctrinal solutions to these questions about how to integrate these various strands of the biblical witness about the concept "Spirit," it is little wonder that the Holy Spirit has been a relatively neglected theme in Christian theology.

Countless theological interpretations of the Trinitarian formula have been offered with an eye toward dealing with these questions. I find none more helpful than a proposal by Augustine. It basically represents the perspective of this volume. Picking up the notion of the Spirit as God's self-knowledge (1 Cor. 2:10-11), the Spirit was understood by Augustine as the bond between Father and Son.[5] It is in this sense that the Spirit *proceeds* from the Father, creating the Father's fellowship with the Son. This is consistent with the Old Testament notion of Yahweh's Spirit as a creative Spirit (Ps. 33:6; Gen. 1:2). The Spirit is that in God which creates fellowship and self-knowledge between Father and Son.

With this supposition it becomes possible to account for how the Spirit could be eternally with God and still be particularly associated with Christ and the eschatological fulfilment. If it is through the Spirit that God creates fellowship, both within the Godhead and through creation with humanity, then it would follow quite logically that God's way of reestablishing fellowship with humanity through Christ would be by the Spirit's work. However, since the Spirit could only function in this way after Christ had atoned for sin, it follows that the Spirit's work must be preceded by Christ—proceed from Christ.[6] Since this is a radically new kind of fellowship created by the Spirit, it is fair to say that the Spirit's work in establishing fellowship through Christ is eschatological in character.

The Augustinian approach to the problem of integrating the Holy Spirit's relation to the Trinity with the biblical witness' apparent subordination of the Spirit to the Son underlines the importance of the final, most recent ecumenical development in the Trinity doctrine and the doctrine of the Holy Spirit. We are led to consider the issue of the *filioque controversy*.

The filioque controversy was occasioned by the Western church's consideration of these issues of the biblical witness' apparent subordination of the Holy Spirit to the Son in light of the conclusions reached by the church about the Trinity doctrine. Sometime after the Council of Nicea the Western church began adding an amendment to the Nicene Creed in liturgical settings. In regard to the Holy Spirit the phrase was added that the Spirit "proceeds from the Father *and the Son*" (*ex Patre Filioque procedit*). The ensuing controversy has been termed the filioque controversy because the Latin term *filioque* means "and the Son." The controversy was over whether or not the church could legitimately add to the Creed this notion that the Spirit proceeds from the Son as well as from the Father. This amendment was well ingrained in the Western church by A.D. 883, but was not the practice in the Eastern church. The ensuing controversy between these two segments of the church over the next two hundred years was one of the factors which led to Eastern Orthodoxy's schism with the Roman Catholic Church in A.D. 1054. The amended version of the Creed, including the *filioque*, received eventual formal ratification in the Western church at the Council of Lyons in A.D. 1274.[7]

There are some important issues at stake in this affirmation that the Spirit proceeds not just from the Father but also from the Son. In fact the issues were perhaps important enough to warrant the schism between the Eastern and Western churches. (Virtually all creedal denominations found in this country have opted for the Western church's inclusion of the *filioque*.) The issues at stake for the Western church may be summarized under two rubrics. They relate to points already made about the work of the Holy Spirit and the content of what the Spirit reveals in relation to Christ.[8]

First, the church was committed to the fact that the Spirit could reveal nothing other than what was given in and consistent with Christ's revelation. If the Spirit proceeds from the Father alone that might imply that the Spirit had a different mission than that of the Son. Thus to protect the Christocentric character of the Holy Spirit's work, the church also had to affirm that the Spirit proceeds from Father and Son.

The second rationale for affirming the *filioque* is that the unity of the Godhead is at stake. The church, it is argued, affirms that the content of God's revelation is always the same. Thus it follows that if the Spirit is revealed to us as the Spirit of the Father, it must also be the Spirit of the Son, else God would be divided. If the Spirit were divided, God would be other than is revealed in Christ. In that case the peace and security of the gospel would be forfeit. We could never be sure that Jesus' Word was God's final Word to us.

For the Eastern church the issues are no less important. The problem with the *filioque* is that it is an unauthoritative addition to the original Nicene Creed. As such the Western church has taken upon itself to overturn the authority of an ecumenical council. Subjectivism and clerical will-to-power are the only logical outcomes of embracing the *filioque*. Furthermore, it is argued by the Eastern church, denial of the *filioque* need not compromise the Christocentric character of the Spirit's work. The problem with the Western church has been its failure to recognize the difference between the "theological/inter-Trinitarian" substantial proceeding of the Spirit from the Father and the "economic/impartation" of the Spirit to humankind proceeding through the work of the Son.[9] The former need not negate the latter.

The issues at stake in the church's schism over the *filioque* are quite substantial. The disagreement is not merely a play on words. Yet when one considers the Eastern church's valid intentions perhaps we can concede that the schism may not be irreparable. It may be that one side of the controversy offers a clearer, more coherent treatment of the subject. Although this does not preclude that both sides allow the church to affirm the biblical witness in regards to the Spirit's eschatological-Christocentric work and eternal fellowship with the Father.

The preceding discussion has integrated all the strands in the biblical witness pertaining to the concept "Spirit" except one: how does the Holy Spirit (and Yahweh's Spirit) relate to the human spirit? We turn to this question at the conclusion of our discussion, because it provides further insights into the significance of this doctrine in our daily lives. (One additional tension, which will be more appropriately considered in the chapter on baptism and the sacraments, should be noted. We shall discuss at that time what the temporary gift of the Spirit to the Old Testament leaders has to do with the permanent gift of the Holy Spirit to all believers. I believe we can show that these two biblical themes relate to each other as ordination relates to the baptismal lifestyle given to every Christian.)

We have seen that the Holy Spirit is significant for us insofar as the Spirit makes Christ present to us. In giving us Christ the Holy Spirit brings us life and salvation. The new identity I have in Christ through union with him and through my baptism is all the work of the Holy Spirit. In short, the Holy Spirit is the agent of reconciliation.

This raises the issue of how completely dependent we are upon the Spirit. Is there some sense in which human beings have a necessary role in appropriating what God has done? How does the Holy Spirit's work relate to the integrity of our own actions (the human spirit)? Since no orthodox Christian would deny that redemption is God's work, our interest in these questions will inevitably focus on the status of faith. Granted the fact that God through the Holy Spirit works salvation, are human beings free to accept or reject the divine offer? How does the Holy Spirit work in relation to the human spirit? Basically three responses to these sets of questions can be identified.[10]

One way of understanding faith is to regard it in terms of *autonomy*. On these grounds we are free to accept or reject the divine offer of reconciliation. Faith is our own work. Such a view has been affirmed by some theologians throughout history.[11] It is found in the contemporary church more than we might like to admit. Yet it is not ultimately a viable option. It is semi-Pelagian in character. It envisions a kind of divine-human partnership.

Heteronomy is a second way of understanding faith. This view regards faith as totally God's work. The Holy Spirit is understood to violate the human spirit in bringing about faith. Sometimes theologians who opt for predestination embrace this view. Certainly one can find Martin Luther tending toward an understanding of faith like this at some points; God works faith against our will.[12] However, it seems difficult systematically to integrate this view with the many biblical exhortations to have faith (see Mark 16:16; James 1:22ff.).

A third approach, *theonomy*, seeks to integrate the best elements of the preceding two approaches. On this basis faith is understood totally as God's work, yet accomplished in such a way that the Holy Spirit works through the structures of human existence. This view is evident in the sermon which follows and has been the underlying presupposition of all that has been said about faith in this volume. (The call to "come as you are" in the sermon on justification must be understood in this way. It implies the affirmation that accepting our acceptance through faith is God's work in us. Yet God works in us in such a way that we really come.)

This integration of the Holy Spirit and human spirit is suggested by Augustinian and Pauline understandings of the concept "Spirit." Recall that both regarded the Spirit as divine self-knowledge which creates fellowship (1 Cor. 2:10-11). This correlation between self-knowledge and relatedness to others is fundamental to the concept of personal identity that I have articulated. Since there is no essential self, one cannot exist or know oneself apart from interaction with others.

On these grounds one might understand sin as the unwillingness or inability to find one's identity in relating to God. In that sense faith can never be humanity's work. Yet we never lose our human spirit in the sense that we continue to have our identity defined by our relatedness to others. Faith, however, must be brought about in us by the Holy Spirit. Only the Spirit can redirect our relatedness to God so that God, through Word and sacrament, comes to define our self-knowledge and our identity.[13] The Holy Spirit relates to the human spirit in the sense that the Spirit works through our creaturehood to accomplish and create all that is good. Such a theonomous approach allows Christians to affirm God's complete responsibility for salvation but in such a way that the structures of human creaturehood are also affirmed.

The following sermon seeks to express the peace and security which this insight about how God works through humanity can offer to us. It will witness to the fact that the church does well to struggle to resolve the tensions and puzzles posed for it by the biblical witness to the concept of the Holy Spirit. We shall be reminded how this doctrine makes God more real by providing us with a sense of Christ's shaping and transforming presence in our lives.

§

Text: 1 John 4:13–21
(*Preached in blue-collar congregation.*)

You know, kids can ask the darndest questions, and some of those questions can really put parents on the spot. Do those of you who are parents now ever have occasions when your kids have just stumped you?

With that in mind, let me tell you a story. One day little Johnny sat in Sunday school and learned all about the Holy Spirit, sometimes called the Holy Ghost. At lunch that day Johnny said to his parents: "We learned all about the Holy Ghost in Sunday school today, but I still don't understand about the Holy Ghost. Does he go around haunting houses and scaring people like other ghosts?" "Ah, ah, ah . . .", replied Johnny's parents. They never did answer the question, and little Johnny went away thinking that maybe the Holy Spirit really did haunt people.

A few years went by, and Johnny was a little older. For quite a while he had begun to doubt that there really were such things as ghosts. One day after talking with some friends about whether ghosts really did exist, he came home that night and asked his parents what they thought about ghosts and goblins and the like. His parents, who were just ordinary folks like you and me, told him they did not believe in ghosts. For a while that made Johnny feel good, then he began thinking. Finally at dessert be blurted out: "But Mom and Dad, if there's no ghosts, does that mean that there's no Holy Ghost?"

Perhaps you have never been involved in a situation like this. As a child you may never have asked such questions. Or maybe your parents gave you the most theologically correct explanation that is possible about who the Holy Spirit is. Yet somehow the doctrine of the Holy Spirit is a dimension of our faith that most Christians find very difficult to understand. Generally speaking, we really do not know what in the world the Holy Spirit is or does. We talk about and confess the Spirit in the creed. But just the same, does the Holy Ghost or the Holy Spirit really have any impact on our faith? Does it really make a difference? If we threw the concept of the Holy Spirit out of Christianity, would it make any difference in the way we live our everyday lives?

There is something about the attitudes of our society and about the nature of Chrisitan theology which makes belief in the Holy Spirit difficult to understand. How can we believe in the Holy Spirit or disbelieve for that matter? We do not have enough evidence to know who the Spirit is. Yet in today's lesson from John's first epistle (1 John 4:13–21) we learn that the Holy Spirit is our *proof* that God loves us. That is right; the Holy Spirit proves to us that we dwell in God.

Thus when we talk about the Holy Spirit we are dealing with one of the most important dimensions of Christian faith because we have our assurance, our security in the work of the Holy Spirit. Yet still the Christian community does not seem clear about who or what the Holy Spirit is.

I want to make it clear to you, friends, that I am not picking on the theological astuteness of the members of this parish. Our lack of understanding is typical of Christians all over the church and throughout history. It is a problem for two reasons: first, in some periods of its history the church thought it could get along without asserting the divinity of the Holy Spirit, and secondly, our modern world view makes us very suspicious of ghosts and spirits, and so, presumably suspicious of the Holy "Ghost." The result in either case is that the Holy Spirit comes to be seen as having little place in our lives.

In light of all this I think it is time to devote a sermon to the doctrine of the Holy Spirit. Now you will notice that when I refer to the Holy Spirit, I never say Holy Ghost. The reason for this is that in no language except English is the Holy Spirit called the Holy Ghost. In Greek, the language in which the New Testament was written, the word used is πνεῦμα, that is Spirit. In Latin *Spiritus Sanctus* means the Holy Spirit. In German, it is *Heilige Geist*. And *Geist* does *not* mean ghost; it means Spirit. What is unfortunate about the English language is that somehow the concept of Spirit gets confused with the idea of a ghost. That is unfortunate because the Holy Spirit bears no similarity at all to a ghost. The Holy Spirit does not haunt people or work in a white sheet. The concept of the Spirit has to do, *not* with something mysterious or strange, but rather with something common and ordinary. You see, the word "spirit" in the Bible refers to the active element in human life. You have heard the word used that way. We say of people who are persistent or hard-working, always on the go, that they have spirit. Kids who have a little bit of the devil in them are also said to have spirit. From this it follows that the Holy Spirit is the active element in the divine life, grabbing hold of our everyday lives in order to sanctify them, to make them holy. That is nothing like our idea of a ghost! No, the Holy Spirit is not like a ghost.

This brings us to the question of how the Holy Spirit works in our everyday lives. First we must reconsider the Trinity and recognize that each of the three persons of the Trinity has a function, a job to do. The Father is Creator of the world and continues to create and sustain it. The Son helped in creation and then, as Jesus Christ, became human and saved us. Yet now Jesus has returned to the Father in heaven. Thus it is up to the Holy Spirit to be present among us. The Holy Spirit is God's presence with us right here and now, and God *is* with us right now *here*. Oh, don't look for God underneath the first pew or behind that post, my friends; you will not find God. Yet God is present with us right here.

This appreciation of God's presence through the Holy Spirit is an important and highly relevant insight. It speaks to many of us because we have gotten this idea that God sits somewhere out there on the clouds, not involved in our lives, perhaps not even caring. Yet if we know that God is truly with us, right beside us, that God knows us better than we know ourselves, then God becomes a lot more personal, and so a lot easier to love. If God is "out there" we cannot converse, not really. Yet if God is with me in everything I do, then love is possible. I can really love God. The doctrine of the Holy Spirit helps make God more accessible and so more real to us.

Additionally, the doctrine of the Holy Spirit offers us the proof that we dwell in God and that God dwells in us. This is John's point in today's lesson (1 John 4:13). Then John goes on to say that if anyone acknowledges that Jesus is the Son of God then that person dwells in God (1 John 4:15). In other words, we can only say that Jesus is the Son of God because we have the Holy Spirit. That is, the Holy Spirit is responsible for *our* faith. The Spirit creates our faith. Does that sound strange? Yet if we think about it together, maybe we will come to appreciate that this is not so strange after all. Indeed, it is a source of joy and comfort for Christians.

We have spoken a good deal about sin since I became your pastor. By now I hope that most of you have come to realize that sin is not just wrong actions. Sin is selfishness, pride, and excessive preoccupation with oneself and one's projects. All of us are marked by this kind of sin and selfishness in all we do. Even in the very best of our deeds we are looking, though unconsciously, to get something out of it for ourselves. Attending church, trying to be a good parent, helping kids, visiting old folks, preaching a sermon—all these good deeds are marred by sin and selfishness.

Despite such harsh realism, the Christian faith does not encourage us to throw our arms into the air and cry, "Sin, sin, everything is sin. " Not at all! Christian faith gladly affirms that there are good things in life. People hear the Word of God through my sinful mouth; people find pleasure watching selfish, greedy athletes perform; children get care and attention as a result of their parents' desire to see them succeed because it makes them feel good; wives and husbands receive love from each other because each needs to be needed. The list of such actions is endless. The point is that there is good in the world and that this good comes about in spite of our selfishness and evil. Yet the biblical witness also asserts that all this good, all the good there is in the world, is really God's work.

If God's kingdom is served by what I am doing, I cannot take the credit for it. It is God's work. In the words of Paul: "it is no longer I who live, but Christ who lives in me" (Gal. 2:20). Who is this Christ in me? It is God present to us right now in the person of the Holy Spirit.

What have you done lately that was nice for somebody else? What kindness have you shown? No matter what, it was not you who did it, not really. It was the Holy Spirit working through you.

I know that this is hard to accept, so chew on it awhile. Take it home today and think about it. If the Holy Spirit is God's presence in our everyday lives, then the Spirit is present with us in everything. Nothing we do in faith is done alone, without the Holy Spirit. Thus anything good we do *has* to be the Spirit working in us.

What does the idea of the Holy Spirit have to tell us about our faith? It has been said of twentieth-century Christians that we believe in miracles but live in a world without them. God seems so far away, so uninvolved in our lives. Yet what if *every* good gift in life—your family, the church, your friends, the clothes you wear, the food you eat—what if all these things were understood as coming from God? What if every good thing that ever happened to you was really God's work? We already know that the Christian doctrine of creation affirms this. But the Holy Spirit makes us aware that God is still personally involved in this creative work. It is the Holy Spirit working through us who leads to all the good in the world. Of course, the Spirit can neither be felt nor seen. Neither does the Spirit talk directly to us, whispering in our ear. Yet we can tell God's Spirit has been here by the good that has been done. That good is all God's work. Thus the Holy Spirit, by working good among us, is always pointing us back toward God, reminding us that in the end God really is the source of our life—that without God there is no good at all. The Holy Spirit is God among us here and now, God in our very midst. Amen.

Chapter Eleven
THE CHURCH

Two terms used by the New Testament to designate the church, *ecclesia* (ἐκκλησία) and *body of Christ*, (σῶμα Χριστοῦ), summarize all that needs to be said about this doctrine. The term *ecclesia* literally means "called out." It has its roots in ancient Greece where it referred to an assembly of citizens "called out" to elect magistrates. Paul may have borrowed the term from Athens and applied it to Christian gatherings as a way of communicating the fact that Christians have been "called out" from the world and the world's people (See 1 Thess. 2:14).[1] The church as *ecclesia* is "called out" in the sense that membership in the church entails a radically new mode of existence. As such, the term *ecclesia* connotes the church's eschatological character as a community that has been "called out" of the old realities to give witness to the new reality of God's kingdom.

The term "body of Christ" conveys another dimension of the church's character. It provides a powerful witness to the fact that Christians are bound together in a kind of organic community in which everything is shared in common (Rom. 12:4–8; I Cor. 12:12ff.). To say that the church is the body of Christ (see Eph. 1:23; Col. 1:18) is to say more than that the church is institutionally organized. Rather the body of Christ is a living reality. The image conveys the fact that Christians are united to each other and to Christ as a vine is to a branch (John 15:3–5). All that Christ has is given to the church, to Christians, and all that they have is to be shared with each other (see 2 Cor. 1:5ff.; Rom. 6:1ff.). The best analogy for expressing this kind of relationship among members of the body is the Christian view of marriage: two become one. The partners in a marriage share all they have, so that the best qualities and characteristics of each seem to rub off on and be reflected in the life of the other. So it is with the relationship between Christians and Christ in the body (Eph. 5:25–30). Thus to refer to the church as body of Christ is to emphasize the church's character as a community.

This brief word study of the terms *ecclesia* and "body of Christ" has provided us with an understanding of the church about which all Christians can agree. The two terms taken together convey the idea that the church is an "eschatological community"—a community which bears witness to God's ultimate purpose for the world and which transcends the limitations of space and time. (The term *ecclesia* is used in the New Testament at some points to refer to the universal church; see Acts 15:3; 2 Cor. 1:1; Gal. 1:13).

The study of these two terms also provides insights into an age-old question about the church: is its development legitimately grounded in the ministry of Jesus or must we regard the church as a later development brought about by the unexpected delay of Jesus' second coming?

The application of the term *ecclesia* to the early Christian community clearly suggests that the idea of the church was the result of the delay in Christ's coming. Perhaps the earliest application of the term is found in 1 Thessalonians 1:1. There it is closely tied to Paul's counsel in regards to the delay in Christ's coming again (1 Thess. 4:13ff.). Because of this delay, some order among Christians is necessary so that they might "build one another up" (1 Thess. 5:11). Thus the evolution of church order and fixed forms of ministry are clearly related to the early church's need to redefine its eschatological expectations (see 1 Thess. 5:12–13).

Of course this is not to say that early Christians ever forfeited their faith in the eschatological fulfilment (Christ's second coming or *parousia*). Rather than compensating for Christ's failure to return, Christians came to see their mission as that of celebrating and proclaiming the presence of him who promised to return. His presence and the fellowship he had created with believers was no longer directly accessible after his resurrection. His presence could only be celebrated among Christians and in the worship forms of their community (i.e., the sacraments). Thus early Christian understandings of both the church and the sacraments came to be intimately connected with a celebration of the presence of Christ and his eschatological message.[2] From the earliest Christian period, then, the doctrines of the church and the sacraments came to be associated with eschatological witness.

The implications for contemporary ministry of the eschatological witness associated with the doctrines of the church and sacraments will be developed more fully in the chapter on eschatology. For the present it is sufficient to note that the term *ecclesia*, which conveys being "called out" from the world, was an excellent term to convey the church's understanding of itself as people providing an eschatological witness. This association of eschatological themes with the New Testament understanding of the church is further certified by the identification of the church as the *people of God* (see Rom. 9:25–26; Titus 2:14) or the *Israel of God* (Gal. 6:16). These terms serve to identify the church as the eschatological fulfilment of the Old Testament.

Of course it should be noted that this correlation of the reality of the church with eschatological themes in no way connotes an absolute identification of the church with the kingdom of God as an eschatological fulfilment of all Jesus had proclaimed. There is ecumenical agreement about this matter.[3] The realities of ordinary congregational life in the institutional church make it all too obvious that the eschaton has not been fully realized in the church. If the church's actual practice in all dimensions were a herald of things to come, it would perhaps be preferable to remain a citizen of the old order. Nevertheless even the New Testament witness confirms that the development of the church is intimately related to the Christian community's coming to terms with the delay of Christ's second coming.

This appreciation of what is connoted by the term *ecclesia*, coupled with the fact that the church is rarely mentioned in the

Synoptic Gospels, suggests that Jesus did not always have the church in mind during the course of his ministry. To the degree that the theological development of the doctrine of the church was a consequence of the delay of Christ's second coming, the idea of the church cannot have been part of Jesus' ministry. His ministry had already been concluded before the period in which the delay of his second coming, and so the church, became issues for reflection. However, the application of the term "body of Christ" to the church suggests that the church is in fact a legitimate development of Jesus' ministry. It is already prefigured in his relationship with his disciples.

Recall that to identify the church as the body of Christ is to refer to the fellowship that exists between Christians and Christ in the church. The Gospel accounts make it clear that Jesus did not view his disciples merely as theological students, but rather as those who were intimately related to him (see Luke 22:28–30; Mark 2:19), who shared all that he had (Mark 6:7–13; Matt. 10:1; Luke 9:1–6).[4] The theme of table fellowship among Jesus and the disciples, so prominent in the Gospel accounts (see Matt. 9:14–15; Mark 2:15; Luke 14:7ff.), serves to undergird the theme of fellowship among Jesus and his followers as a central core of Jesus' ministry. (Subsequently in chapter thirteen we shall see that even the Lord's Supper must be regarded in this way. It is Jesus continuing table fellowship with the disciples after his ascension.) Thus fellowship in the church among Christians and Christ, connoted by the identification of the church as the body of Christ, was a central element in Jesus' ministry.

This data serves to indicate that the church is the work of Jesus even though he did not always have the church and its structures in mind.[5] It can be argued that even the subsequent association of the doctrine of the church with eschatology was grounded in Jesus' ministry. His emphasis on the kingdom of God and its coming (see Matt. 4:23; Mark 1:14–15) entails that the fellowship created through this ministry would have an eschatological flavor.

It is evident that although the doctrine of the church did develop as a result of issues raised for early Christians after Jesus' ascension, there can be no doubt that the church's formulation of this doctrine affirmed nothing which was not already implicit in Jesus' ministry. His ministry included fellowship between him and his followers, fellowship which had eschatological overtones. The later New Testament idea of the church as eschatological community logically follows from this.

An appreciation of the legitimate connection between Jesus' ministry and the doctrine of the church has important implications for us living in an era when the gospel can be heard via television and radio. There is a tendency to think that one can be a Christian apart from the church. We have seen, though, that if Jesus' ministry is a paradigm, one cannot be a Christian apart from fellowship with Christ and other Christians. Thus the church has a biblical basis for critiquing all antiecclesiastical attitudes in contemporary society.

To this point we have dealt with matters about which most Christians can agree. However, the doctrine of the church has at times been a major source of disagreement among Christians. Basically these disagreements focus on the issue of how to identify the eschatological community. On what basis can it be determined that a fellowship of Christians is in fact legitimately the church?

In a sense all Christians have agreed upon a common starting point for this discussion. The Nicene Creed identifies these common presuppositions. A gathering or fellowship of believers is only the church if it is one (with all Christians), holy, catholic (in the sense of being worldwide or universal), and apostolic. In fact, however, the meaning of these marks of the true church varies from tradition to tradition depending upon the other means these various traditions use in identifying the church. We shall proceed with a brief discussion of the various ways in which the church has been identified.

Many Protestants, notably Baptists and Mennonites, identify the church in terms of its members, as the assembly of the converted.[6] On this basis the church may be deemed holy in virtue of the holiness of its members. It is held together in unity with all who believe likewise. It is apostolic insofar as the faith of the apostles is present in its members. The great strength of this view of the church is that it entails an emphasis on Christian life and living the faith. One cannot be part of the church unless one meets certain membership expectations in regards to spirituality. The problem associated with such a viewpoint is that it can lead to a kind of legalist-Pelagian mentality unless it is made very clear that the church's members have faith only in virtue of God's theonomous activity in them. Another problem is that such an emphasis upon the holiness or spirituality of the church's members can lead to a kind of *sect* mentality. Because the members of the church are holy they fail to interact with the profane world for fear of being contaminated by its unholy secularism. The abuses associated with this way of regarding the church's relation to the world are quite obvious. We have already identified them in the chapter on sanctification and so need not reiterate.

A second, more historically venerable way of identifying the church, is held by the Roman Catholic and the Eastern Orthodox traditions. These groups do not define the church in terms of its members, but rather in terms of certain external and visible marks. The church is identified as the congregation of the faithful united by the sacraments and under the authority of the episcopacy (body of bishops).[7] There is strong precedent for this understanding in early Christian theology. The third-century Bishop of Carthage, Cyprian, was one of the first to define the church and its unity in terms of bishops, who are the successors of the apostles.[8] Furthermore the view seems biblically based. One can find texts in the New Testament which suggest that the church is founded on the apostles (Matt. 16:18–19; Eph. 2:20; Rev. 21:14) or that it is called into being by baptism (see 1 Cor. 12:12–13).

This view of the church understands the church's unity and catholicity in terms of the visible marks of the sacraments and episcopacy. Precisely because the church has bishops in all the world and celebrates the sacraments everywhere, the church is catholic and one.

A great strength of this view is that it affirms the action of God in creating the church. The church is created by God through the celebration of the sacraments and the authority given the apostles, not by its members through their holiness. In fact this view was articulated in the early centuries in response to the problem raised by the readmission of those believers who had renounced their faith during the period of Roman persecutions. Readmission of the lapsed would damage the ideal of the pure church; the sense in which it is holy had to be redefined.[9] Given this view the church is holy in virtue of its relationship to Christ and the external means of grace (the sacraments) he has given it. Unlike the first view of the church, the focus is on God's act, not on the believer's response.

This second way of identifying the church does entail a high view of the ministry. The church is founded upon a special group of Christians, the clergy. They have received special authority through their ordination. Particularly bishops have this authority in virtue of being in a direct line of succession from the apostles. Thus the church is deemed to be apostolic insofar as its leadership holds its authority on behalf of the apostles. Apostolic succession in the episcopacy, through the laying on of hands at the clergy's ordination or installation by a cleric already in the apostolic line of succession, is a given among Christians who hold this understanding of the church. In Roman Catholicism this leads quite logically to the affirmation of papal primacy. The Pope is most eminent in the church because he exercises the authority given to him through the apostolic line of succession, which belongs properly to the foremost of the apostles, Peter. This is a credible view which is not easily dismissed. Peter's preeminent role in the early church seems to be substantiated by biblical sources (see Matt. 16:18; Acts 1:15).

Although it has much to commend itself, the problem with this second way of identifying the church is that it can imply clericalism, an unhealthy distinction between clergy and laity. In response several Protestant bodies, namely the Reformed and Lutheran traditions, have opted for a similar objective emphasis in identifying the church, but without reference to the episcopacy as one of the church's external marks. Thus Lutherans and Presbyterians identify the church as "the assembly of all believers among whom the gospel is preached in its purity and the sacraments are administered rightly."[10] To these two marks, the Reformed Presbyterian tradition has sometimes added a third—discipline. Thus the church is identified by the pure preaching of the Word, the right administration of the sacraments, and discipline.[11]

Both forms of this third way of identifying the church exhibit strengths similar to the second view, without the dangers of espousing clericalism. The objective character of God's act in creating and upholding the church is affirmed. There seems to be biblical support for such a view (see Eph. 5:25–27). As such, the church's unity and catholicity are established by its external marks. Christians are in unity with Christians all over the world wherever the Word is properly preached and the other marks of the church are rightly practiced. Likewise the church's holiness is not dependent on the holiness or spirituality of its members. It is holy in virtue of Christ's fellowship with and action in the community, which make it holy. Even the church's apostolicity is defined not in virtue of its clergy's being in the line of apostolic succession. Rather it is apostolic in virtue of preaching the same gospel as the apostles did.

The disagreements, then, between Christians about the doctrine of the church are ultimately reducible to the matter of which of these various ways of identifying the church a given tradition holds. The Christian community disagrees about the criteria for determining the true church, not about the reality of the church as an eschatological fellowship between Christ and the faithful. In fact, when one studies these various options for identifying the church more closely, the areas of agreement seem even more pronounced. There is hope that the doctrine of the church need not be the rationale for Christians to remain separated. These other points of agreement, which may ultimately serve to facilitate ecumenical rapprochement should be noted.

Of course it is true that the understanding of the role of the ordained ministry in constituting the church differs in the various alternatives we have studied. This in turn suggests that the various Christian communities are also divided over their understanding of the office of the ministry. Those traditions which opt for identifying the church in terms of the episcopacy (Roman Catholic, Eastern Orthodox, Anglican) would seem to have a high view of the ministry. That is to say the pastor/priest is understood as set apart, standing over against the community. By contrast one would expect those traditions which opt for other means of identifying the church to have a lower view of the ministry. Here the pastor is not placed above the church but is regarded as a member of it. These are certainly the classic stereotypical understandings of the difference between Protestant and Catholic views of the ministry.

In fact, however, ecumenical agreement is implied in the various Christian traditions' view of the ministry in such a way that the different understandings of the church we have discussed need not divide Christians. This agreement is best summarized by a recent ecumenical dialogue. The participants conclude "that the office of Ministry stands over-against the community as well as in it and that the ministerial office represents Christ and His over-againstness to the community only insofar as it gives expression to the Gospel."[12]

This definition of the ministry is implicit in the various Christian communities though it might not seem to be the case at first glance. It is most clearly evident in the Lutheran and Reformed traditions. Each regards the pastor as part of the universal priesthood of believers, chosen by the church for the sake of good order.[13] Yet each in turn regards the office of ministry as essential to the nature of the church, divinely instituted and so set over against the members of the church.[14] Likewise both dimensions of the ministry are implicit in the other Protestant traditions more influenced by pietism. These traditions tend to emphasize the minister's complete identification with the community, as a reaction against all hierarchical views of the ministry. The pastor is regarded as just another member of the universal priesthood. Yet in effect the pastor is usually set over against the laity by these traditions, insofar as he or she is seen as someone with a deeper spirituality.

Even in those traditions which define the church in terms of the episcopacy and opt for apostolic succession, the two dimensions of the ministry are not totally negated. To be sure the emphasis in these traditions is upon the pastor/priest standing over against the church, insofar as the office defines the church. Yet when we recall that the sacraments also identify the church for these traditions and that one becomes a member of the clergy through the sacrament of ordination, it follows that the office of ministry is derived and chosen from the church. There can be no priest who was not part of the church prior to ordination. Thus the priest stands over against the church only in virtue of being part of the church and receiving its sacraments.

It is evident by now that all Christian traditions implicitly affirm a two-dimensional view of the ministry—the pastor as both part of the church yet exercising authority over it. Pastors in all traditions find themselves caught in a tension between the leadership styles and expectations associated with each dimension. Although we cannot presently elaborate on this matter, suffice it to say that this can be a creative tension. It provides pastors with the freedom both to identify with the laity and encourage a mutual, shared ministry, yet also to exercise authority over the congregation for the sake of proclaiming the gospel.[15]

This reference to the proclamation of the gospel returns us to the second point of agreement among Christians in regards to the doctrine of the church. Despite the different ways of identifying the church (in terms of Word, sacrament, episcopacy, spirituality of believers, etc.), there is a common reality by which the church is defined in all cases. In each instance there is agreement that the gospel constitutes the church.

Of course the idea that the gospel constitutes the church is explicitly endorsed by those traditions which identify the church in terms of Word and sacraments. Yet this theme is no less present in the Roman Catholic and Eastern Orthodox traditions. To say, as they do, that the sacraments and ministry identify the church presupposes that the gospel is working through these means to establish the church. Indeed the teaching authority of the episcopacy is even subordinated to the gospel insofar as its sole purpose is to serve the gospel. Likewise in those traditions which identify the church in terms of the spirituality of its members, the gospel is implicitly regarded as founding the church. For the spirituality of Christians cannot create itself. It is created and nurtured by the gospel. Thus if the spirituality of Christians upholds the church and this spirituality was created by the gospel, it must follow that the gospel is the foundation of the church. All Christians affirm this last point. The differences among Christians in the means they use to identify the church appear not to be differences in kind, but rather differences in emphasis. Ultimately all agree that the gospel holds the church together. The prospects for Christian unity on the issues covered in this chapter seem very realistic.

This last point about the gospel holding together the church and its fellowship warrants further consideration. It speaks to the question of what the church has to offer contemporary human beings. When people raise the question of who needs the church, Christians have something to say. The church offers a cohesive community held together by the gospel.

At this point a few brief comments about communities are helpful. All communities require something to hold them together. When a community forms, the norms which hold the community together acquire such authority that they become internalized by the community's citizens and shape their identity. Thus most Americans venerate democracy because our community's democratic norms have shaped their identities. This phenomenon happens also in the Christian community. Its principal norm, the gospel, calls the community into being and shapes the identities of the community's members. Why do we need the church? It is the only community in which we can receive our Christian identity.

In view of the contemporary cultural dynamics we noted in the first chapter (narcissism and the consequent loss of personal identity), it is apparent how important a resource the church is for ministry today. In a society where people are searching for identity, the church is a community where people can find themselves (have their identity created by the gospel). The church is a community where people come to be conformed to Christ (see chapter eight) and united with each other. Christians whose identities have been shaped by membership in the church cannot be themselves any longer apart from Christ or apart from their neighbor. Christians cannot be themselves any longer apart from these relationships any more than I can be myself apart from the relationship I have with my wife and family or apart from the love of sports which my community has instilled in me.

The gospel sets Christians free from the mad chase for identity. It sets them free to live the gospel and in so doing to participate in God's ongoing project of creating good. The church's importance is that it functions as a kind of resting place, a refuge for Christians on this journey. In the church we find a community which is our home. It is a community which can nourish and refresh us.

Why do we need the church? The following sermon seeks to address this question. Implicit in what is said is the idea that we need the church because participation in it, being nurtured by its norms, strengthens and renews the identity given us in baptism. In the church we participate in a community which is held together by that which makes us who we are. The more we are a part of it, the more our lives are profoundly shaped by the gospel. In yet one more way, though, we do need the church. Twentieth-century believers need the eschatological fellowship the church offers us with Christ and each other. In the church we have each other to lean on when we are uncertain of our identity and uncertain in our faith. At a time of so much uncertainty the church offers us the security of fellowship with Christ and with each other so that we are strengthened to risk creating new good in the world. Christians need the church to be themselves!

§

Text: Acts:2:1–21
(*Preached in small, rural parish.*)

You all know that we are celebrating a birthday today, right? It is a very special birthday, the birthday of the church. Today is Pentecost, the day the very first Christians received the Holy Spirit. That gift got them so excited that they ran out into the street and started telling everybody God's good news. And wonder of wonders, people believed them, and thousands were baptized. The Christian church was born that Pentecost day.

Since this is the day the church as we know it had its start, I think we ought to pay some attention to the "birthday child." I propose we talk about, think about, and even pray about the church today. I think my proposal makes particularly good sense because today is also confirmation Sunday. Part of what our young adults here are promising today is that they want to claim their baptism as their own. As such, they also lay claim to membership in Christ's body. Today, confirmands, you become adult members of the church of Jesus Christ, and I want to tell you all what you are getting into. What is the church? What does it have to offer us citizens of the late twentieth century?

Those of you who have been active in the church for years know it can be quite frustrating at times. It makes you wonder whether we really need the church, whether it isn't Christianity's greatest liability. Quite often it does seem like the church is losing ground. Certainly most of the mainline churches in our country are declining in membership. Additionally the church is not having as much of an impact on all our lives as we might wish. In spite of all our work, it certainly seems like the church is going downhill. This kind of frustration is turning many people off.

The problem is particularly poignant in Western nations it seems like the church (and Christianity) is a one-hour thing on Sundays. Even some of us who put in more than that one hour a week will stop every once in a while and ask, "Hey, how much of a difference is it making in my life? Am I any happier or better off because of my involvement in the church?" Yes, I know that question well. I have asked it more than once myself.

Quite a gloomy picture for a birthday child, don't you think? It is not exactly something to excite our confirmands. See what you're getting into? It sounds pretty depressing. I can tell you that in your life as a member of the church there will be times when you may feel depressed or apathetic. But when you do, I have some good medicine for you. It may restore your confidence in what the church has to offer. The medicine comes from the pen of Martin Luther:

> It is not we who can sustain the church, nor was it our forefathers, nor will it be our descendents. It was and is and will be the One who says: "I am with you always, even unto the end of the world. . . "
>
> For you and I were not alive thousands of years ago, but the church was preserved without us, and it was done by the One [who is Jesus Christ]. . . .
>
> Again we do not do it in our lifetime, for the church is not upheld by us. For we could not resist the devil . . . and the sects and other wicked folk. For us the church would perish before our very eyes and we with it (as we daily prove), were it not for that other man [Jesus Christ] who manifestly upholds the church for us.[16]

These are powerful words, are they not? What a blockbusting message! It is not up to us to keep the church alive, Luther says.

That problem is on God's shoulders and those shoulders are broad enough to sustain us and keep the church afloat, too. These are words of comfort which offer insights about what the church offers us.

When I get down in the dumps about the church, when it seems as if we are all wasting our time because nobody is listening or caring, then Luther's words remind me that the success of the church is not dependent upon me. It is up to God. That feels good; it is a real relief. God's church can get along without us. In the end it will triumph over death and meaninglessness and apathy. That victory has already been guaranteed by Jesus. That is what Easter is all about: Jesus is victor. Thus his body, his church, is in the winner's circle too.

The church is a *winner*, a guaranteed winner. In fact I think that if the church would begin to project itself as victor, sharing in Christ's victory (2 Tim. 4:7-8), then it would begin to remedy its declining influence and help nurture a stronger sense of commitment to its work . Society would then begin to get excited about what we are engaged in. Why? It is a simple matter. People love a winner. That is why the Yankees are so popular today—and why they were in the '50s. (I say that with some bitterness because I stuck with them in the late '60s when they were awful.) *Everybody* loves a winner. Confirmands, today you are joining a guaranteed winner. The fact that everybody loves a winner illustrates how the essence of the church, as sharing in Christ's victory, makes the church exceedingly relevant and attractive to the world in which we live.

Let me spell out this dimension of the church's reality a bit more. You just cannot find the kind of security that church membership offers anywhere else. Marriages fail, children go bad, jobs don't pan out, but the church endures. Good-looks fade, brainpower deteriorates, loved ones die, but God's kingdom is forever. People say to me sometimes: "Why should *I* participate in the church; I can get along fine without it." Yet in times like ours with all the turmoil and rapid change that is going on all around us, the church offers stability. As we seek for something to hold on to, for some security, it is only in the church that we come to belong to the man who once said, "Come unto me all *ye* that labour and are heavy laden, and I will give you rest" (Matt. 11:28 KJV).

It's fun to play for a winner, a joy and not a drudgery. When we join the church, we share in Jesus' victory over sin, death, and evil. We become participants with him in his eternal project of creating new good in the world. And we do it with the assurance that this victory, this creation of good, is not ultimately our responsibility but God's.

What does membership in the church offer us today? Confirmands, today you become full participants in an eternal community which is in tune with the eventual outcome of all history. You and all the rest of us have the joy and security of being part of a community that "knows where it's at!" We are all part of God's winning team.

Of course it is not always that easy to be part of the church. I do not wish to mislead you. Because both we and the church are marred by sin, there are times when it is difficult to believe in God's ultimate victory, times when membership in the church is not particularly significant in our lives. Yet even at these times the church can play a meaningful role.

To be sure, these uncertainties about faith's relevance for daily life and the church's participation in Christ's victory are real problems. They are best remedied by a heroic leap of faith which overcomes our doubts despite what we may be feeling (see Heb. 10:22-23). Yet if the only way to deal with our spiritual doubts were to depend on our own personal faith, then we would all be in trouble. Why? None of us individually has that strong a faith, but together we do. Thus even when the church and Christian faith do not seem relevant in our daily lives, even then the church offers us something indispensable. As the body of Christ the church offers us each other to lean on (see 2 Cor. 1:4-7).

I think this image of what it means for the church to be the body of Christ is nicely evident in Acts 2:44. There we learn how the earliest Christians were communists/socialists in a way. They shared everything in common. This is what Paul means when he calls the church the body of Christ (see Rom. 12:4; 1 Cor. 12:12ff.). When we join the church we become part of Christ's body and share in all that he has. Yet our fellow believers are also part of Christ's body. Thus to belong to his body and share in all that he has means that we share in and belong to each other. What is yours is mine, my fellow members of Christ's body, and what is mine also belongs to you. As the earliest Christians shared all in common and leaned on each other, so it is with us today in the church. We can lean on each other. This is what you can and should expect from all of us, confirmands. This is what you are getting into. It is why God created the church and what it has to offer the world today. When the going gets rough, when it's hard to believe that God's creative ways will be victorious in the world, and when we have difficulty finding life meaningful and faith relevant, then we can lean on each other.

No, perhaps I do not always feel the joy and excitement of participating in Christ's work; perhaps the love of God and a sense of ultimate meaning in life are hidden from me. Yet when I am down, I can lean on some of you who are feeling joy in life and the love of God and are excited about it. If I do that it will be just a bit easier for me to fight my feelings of apathy, despair, and weakness of faith. Being with people who are excited, are feeling God's love, and are confident in the relevance of it all makes God and God's promises a lot more real. Indeed, some of this excitement, confidence, and joy are liable to rub off on the rest of us. Then when the rest of you need it and we who have been in despair are stronger, you can lean on us.

Friends, this is what the church is for. This is what worship, fellowship, and the activities of a congregation are all about. They are occasions for sharing and leaning on each other, occasions for getting so involved in joy and assurance that we come to forget our doubts and sense of purposelessness.

God created the church; the church is still necessary and relevant because none of us is strong enough alone. We are not so faithful that we could be Christians, people with a sense of divine purpose in life, on our own. We need the assurance given by God that the church is his work and that our participation in the church, working with it and him, is ultimately significant. Additionally we need the church because we need each other and the confidence we can give each other to believe that God's promises to us are true. Together, as the body of Christ, we are a winning team. That is why we Christians, and indeed the world, need the church. Confirmands, welcome to the greatest winning team of all time. Amen.

Chapter Twelve
BAPTISM

Consideration of the sacrament of baptism necessitates that we first come to an understanding of the church's view of sacraments in general. Because this topic has been one of the leading causes of schism in the church, our discussion must be sufficiently inclusive to pertain to what all Christians can affirm. Thus as with our discussion of the church, I shall begin by attempting to describe baptism and the sacraments in relation to what is common among most traditions on these topics. Once the commonalities have been appreciated the issues at stake in disagreements among Christians become more readily apparent.

A definition of the sacraments which typifies several traditions is to view them as outward signs with promises attached to them instituted by Christ.[1] Virtually all Christian traditions can accept these three characteristics of a sacrament: (1) an outward sign, (2) a promise attached to the sign, and (3) an institution of Christ. Generally all Christians agree about the nature of the outward sign or rite which constitutes a sacrament. Thus all would agree that eating and drinking bread and wine is the outward sign of the Lord's Supper.

There is also agreement that a sacramental celebration is not negated even if it is conducted by an evil or faithless person. This conclusion was reached as a result of the fourth-century Donatist controversy. *Donatism* held that the church must be purged of clergy who had betrayed their faith under pressures of persecution. The moral pollution of these clerics was thought to invalidate the sacraments they performed. The church eventually rejected this view. In so doing it was largely influenced by Augustine.

Another area of agreement among Christians is that the sacraments are regarded as significant not just because of their divine institution, but also because of the dimension of personal address by God which they add to the life of faith. While the Word of God proclaimed may be addressed to a general audience, Christians who receive the sacraments have the assurance that grace (and the Word) is for them in particular.

Despite these many areas of agreement, however, disagreements have arisen about the issues of what sort of promise is attached to the sacramental sign and what constitutes divine institution. The former issue pertains to the question of whether the sacraments actually give grace (Christ is present in them) or merely symbolize a spiritual reality. The question of what constitutes a sacrament's institution by Christ determines the number of sacraments a given Christian tradition can accept.

In regard to the number of sacraments, the church universally accepts the sacramental status of baptism and the Lord's Supper. In addition to these two, the Roman Catholic and Eastern Orthodox churches have designated five other rites as sacramental: (1) confession, (2) confirmation, (3) ordination, (4) marriage, and (5) extreme unction.[2] Other traditions have provisionally accepted the sacramental status of some of these additional rites.[3]

Actually the system of seven sacraments is a relatively recent development. It was not formally ratified until A.D. 1439 at the Council of Florence. This fact should not militate against the validity of this system, because the additional five rites that have been deemed sacraments are ancient practices of the church which have been esteemed and highly regarded throughout its history. Additionally the doctrine of the sacraments has, generally speaking, developed slowly in all its dimensions. In fact, despite the rapid development of specific means of grace in the church (baptism, eucharist, etc.), early Christian theology did not treat in detail the question of the sacraments in general. Rather its sacramental doctrine emerged from the concrete teaching and practice of particular sacraments. A general doctrine of sacraments did not develop in any form until the medieval period.[4]

I propose to follow the above historical paradigm in this brief discussion of the sacraments. Rather than offering a blanket assessment about the sacramental status of the additional five Roman Catholic sacraments, let us conclude this discussion of the sacraments in general and proceed briefly to examine each particular sacrament (and the validity of its claim to sacramental status).

One rite whose sacramental status is more generally recognized is the sacrament of *confession*. In this rite participants confess their sin to some representative of the church (usually a cleric). This presiding representative in turn pronounces forgiveness/absolution on behalf of Christ.

This rite is founded on the biblical notion of the power of the keys (Matt. 16:19; 18:18; John 21:23). Christ seems to have given the church, through the apostles, the power to forgive or retain the sins of all people. As such, confession is a kind of correlate of both baptism and the proclamation of the gospel. In baptism and through the proclamation of the gospel sin is both condemned and forgiven. Confession merely formalizes this dimension of the church's proclamation. There is no disagreement among Christians, then, about the basic content or intention of the sacrament of confession. Controversy has arisen over the degree to which this dimension of the church's ministry should receive formal structure as a sacrament and what shape that formal structure should take.

The first question in regards to whether confession should be deemed a sacrament is closely related to the matter of whether it has sufficient biblical warrant to indicate its divine institution. In addition to the texts already cited pertaining to the power of the keys, John the Baptist's institution of confession as a correlate of his baptism of repentance has been cited as biblical testimony to the sacrament's divine institution (Matt. 3:6). John is regarded in this case as a precursor of Christ, so that all he institutes is done in Christ's name (John 1:6-8).[5] The question of whether this provides sufficient biblical testimony remains open to debate in the church.

Also at issue in determining confession's sacramental status is the question of whether it actually possesses an outward sign. (Recall that one of the three necessary characteristics of a sacrament is that it has an outward sign.) Since confession can and usually has taken the form merely of a verbal exchange between participant and confessor, its sacramental status has been challenged by some.[6] For the future, hard work needs to be done by theologians and liturgists in identifying the outward sign properly correlated with confession. The biblical idea of a kiss or sign of peace (see 1 Cor. 16:20; 1 Thess. 5:26) might be incorporated in the sacrament. This dimension of physical contact between participant and confessor would provide a biblically-based outward sign for the sacrament, which some say is lacking.

Additionally it may be argued that insofar as confession is celebrated in a worship setting it already possesses an outward sign. The action and movement which happen in worship are this outward sign. There seems to be nothing which would necessarily preclude confession's sacramental status on this basis.

This last consideration suggests the second controversial question over confession's status. This is the question of what structure the sacrament should take. On this point certain historic forms of confession are unacceptable to many Christians. For example, the three stages of confession used by the medieval church (contrition, enumeration, and satisfaction) are unacceptable to Reformation traditions.

In the medieval period the first step in confession was contrition, a feeling of repentance for one's sin. The participants were expected to feel this sorrow for their sin prior to entering confession. Once the rite had begun they moved into the second step, enumeration. In this step penitents were to state verbally every sin that they could recall. This step became a source of real concern for the sixteenth-century Reformers, particularly Luther. He feared that he might omit a few sins in his confession and as a result not receive forgiveness.

The third step in medieval confession was satisfaction. (This step was perhaps most galling to the Reformers.) At this point the penitent was instructed by the confessor to perform certain spiritual tasks which would demonstrate full repentance to God.

There are obvious problems with this structure for the sacrament of confession. A kind of legalism may be connoted in regard to the satisfaction which must be offered to demonstrate full repentance. Absolution, the pronouncement of God's unconditional grace, does not seem to be the final word. Additionally, the idea of satisfaction further connotes that something must be added by us to our baptism in confession. This cannot be accepted by Christians who regard justification as a completed event. Yet, confession may still be rightly understood as a correlate of baptism as long as it is regarded as adding nothing believers do not already possess essentially in their baptism.

As a result of these considerations the formal structure of the sacrament of confession has been rethought. To the degree the rite does reflect that the gospel (absolution) has the final word it can function as a source of comfort and nurture for Christians who seek to live out their baptism.

A second rite whose sacramental status is in dispute is the sacrament of *confirmation*. In this rite the participants confess, confirm, or claim their faith given in baptism. The presiding representative in turn offers a blessing to the confirmand by the laying on of hands (which in some traditions includes anointing with oil).

This rite has its roots in the ancient church where it was originally part of the baptismal service. Subsequent developments in the western church up to the early Middle Ages led to its separation from baptism.[7]

The rite seems to have some biblical foundation. An account in Acts 8:14-17 describes a confirmation celebration led by Peter and John where the Holy Spirit was given to those who had purportedly already been baptized.

This last reference raises two issues in connection with the sacrament. First, it suggests that the biblical basis for confirmation is somewhat flimsy. This continues to be a matter of dispute in the church. Also the issue of what confirmation gives is raised by the text just cited. With the exception of the Orthodox tradition's tendency to regard confirmation (or its equivalent) as the rite in which the Holy Spirit is given, most Christians hold that confirmation merely confirms what is done in baptism. The Spirit is given in the sense that a special *charism* (spiritual gift) is given. What we have in baptism is thus nurtured and strengthened. Given these suppositions, confirmation has played a valid role in nurturing the faith of young Christians in many confessional traditions.

In some respects the third disputed sacramental rite, *ordination*, plays a similar role in the life of the church. Virtually all traditions practice a rite of ordination in order formally to set apart and consecrate persons for service to the church as ordained ministers. There is some biblical reference to this rite (1 Tim. 4:14; Acts 13:3). However, its divine institution is sufficiently unclear on this basis to account for the ongoing disagreement about ordination's sacramental status.

What then is given in ordination? Much like in confirmation, the participant receives a special *charism* from the Holy Spirit. In this case the *charism* is akin to the temporary gift of the Spirit given to Old Testament leaders. This insight provides a helpful way of understanding ordination and of discerning unity in the biblical witness regarding the concept of the Spirit. Just as we may discern coherence in the biblical witness only by positing some relationship between the temporary gift of the Spirit and the permanent gift of the Spirit given to all in baptism, it follows that the special *charism* of ordination is not regarded as superseding or unrelated to baptism. It is in this manner that references in the Old Testament to the special and temporary gift of the Spirit can be integrated with the New Testament's witness. Ordination, therefore, is a sacrament that strengthens ordinands' baptismal gifts so that they may better serve the church.

This last point warrants attention in response to the argument that ordination cannot be a sacrament because it is not given to the whole church, but only to a select few. The best response to be made is that ordination is a rite of the whole church insofar as those who receive it do so to the benefit of the whole church. One might say that ordinands are the elements through whom the Holy Spirit works in giving the church the gift of the Word. Through them grace is given to the whole church.[8]

Marriage might be regarded as a sacrament in much the same way. The institution of marriage provides partners with all sorts of opportunities to live the baptismal life—to deny one's sinful self on behalf of one's partner for the sake of love. The whole church stands to benefit from this. Those who have spent a lifetime dying to self on behalf of their partner will surely be that much more open to serving all their neighbors. Their marriage relationship has so nurtured in them the baptismal life of dying to self that they cannot be themselves apart from serving others. In serving their neighbors, grace is given the whole church through those who participate in the sacrament of marriage.

Traditionally, Ephesians 5:31-34 has been cited in biblical support of marriage's sacramental status. The Eastern Orthodox term for sacrament (*mysterion*) has been kept in view by those who would argue for marriage's sacramental status. Thus when Paul calls marriage a "great mystery" (μέγα μυστήριον), it is argued that he has designated marriage as a sacrament (*mysterion*). In view of such tentative biblical backing it is little wonder that the sacramental status of this rite remains a debatable point in the church universal.

Extreme unction is the fifth and final rite whose sacramental status remains open to question. The sacrament is intended for those who are in peril of death. The dying are to be anointed with oil. In so doing they receive the grace and comfort which is derived from pastoral care. Biblical foundations for this sacrament are found in those texts which speak of anointing the sick or casting out demons (see James 5:14; Acts 28:8; Mark 16:17). Obviously evidence for the actual divine institution of the rite is not as substantive as some of the other disputed sacraments. Thus it is not surprising that even though the dimension of pastoral care associated with extreme unction is ecumenically affirmed, no Protestant has accepted the rite as sacramental.

Several conclusions can be drawn from this brief survey of the five disputed sacraments. First the ambiguities in determining their status must be conceded. These rites have venerable traditions in the history of the church. All of them have some biblical basis. Yet most Protestants have not been persuaded that this is sufficient evidence for their divine institution. The question of what constitutes proper evidence is by no means resolved. (As we shall note below, for example, there is no clear biblical witness for infant baptism. Since Protestants who opt for this rite must appeal to tradition to authenticate the practice, one might ask what would preclude appeal to tradition to authorize the sacramental status of these other rites.) Yet inasmuch as Protestants practice virtually all the rites (presumably as a means of nurturing the Christian life) and to the degree that those opting for their sacramental status believe the rites give nothing not intrinsically given in baptism, the disagreements among Christians on this subject do not seem substantive. Perhaps we should echo the words of the sixteenth-century Reformer, Philip Melanchthon, who wrote, "No intelligent person will quibble about the number of sacraments."[9] At least we might say that the number of sacraments is not a legitimate reason for schism in the church.

Having completed this discussion of the sacraments in general it is now possible to consider the main topic of this chapter, baptism. As with the sacraments in general there is much in regard to baptism about which all Christians can agree. There is agreement about its sacramental status and divine institution in all traditions (see Matt. 28:19; Mark 16:16). There is agreement about the sacrament's outward sign—the application of water in the name of the Triune God. There is also agreement about the meaning of this sign. Its meaning is at least twofold. First, the sign can be understood as a dying to sin (drowning in the water) and resurrection to grace (see Rom. 6:3; Col. 2:12). The sign may also be regarded as signifying a washing for regeneration or a washing away of sin (Titus 3:5; Acts 22:16). Both meanings make it clear that baptism brings about salvation.

Baptism as practiced by the church has its roots in the Old Testament period. Baptism of proselytes (new converts) was a common practice of first-century Judaism. The practice no doubt influenced John the Baptist's practice of a baptism of repentance, which had a direct influence on Jesus himself. This practice of a ritual cleansing was already part of the Old Testament heritage (see Isa. 4:4; Ezek. 36:25–27; Num. 19:1ff.). In this sense one might say that Christian baptism is an eschatological fulfilment of the Old Testament. That the sacrament reflects eschatological themes in this way is not surprising. We have already noted how the doctrines of church and sacraments were formalized in face of the delay of Christ's second coming and the need to keep the hope of his coming alive. Further the eschatological theme is an essential ingredient of the meaning of the baptismal sign. The dying to or washing away of sin implies that one is given a radically new being (a kind of eschatological existence). The gift of a radically new manner of life would seem to be entailed in baptism because baptism is the sacrament of initiation into an eschatological community.

Of course it is not the washing in water alone which brings all this about. In regards to this and all sacraments, Christians are agreed that it is not the elements but the Word of God proclaimed in conjunction with the sacrament that brings about new life. Thus in a very real sense it is the Word of God, God personally, who baptizes (see Titus 3:5).[10] This strong emphasis upon the primacy of God's grace (the doctrine of justification by grace through faith) is witnessed to in baptism and all the sacraments. It is precisely this affirmation that makes it possible for a sacrament to be valid even when administered by an impure person. It is still valid because it is God, not the evil or faithless cleric, who is performing the sacrament.

We have noted four areas of ecumenical agreement about baptism. Christians agree about: (1) baptism's outward sign, (2) the meaning of this sign, (3) the sacrament's eschatological character, and (4) regarding baptism as a work of God. Despite all these common areas of agreement, however, Christians disagree over two related issues: (1) who is to be baptized? and (2) does baptism actually give grace or merely symbolize some inner spiritual transformation? Basically two different alternatives to this set of questions may be identified. (A third area of disagreement, the question of total immersion in baptism, may be quickly dispatched. Although only Baptists insist upon this, most Christian traditions recognize immersion as a most ancient and honorable practice. Some would prefer immersion and practice sprinkling the baptized only for the sake of convenience.[11] This is an issue which shows signs of being resolved in the future.)

Many Protestants, notably Baptists, have maintained that baptism only symbolizes what has already happened to believers through conversion. Baptism then becomes the way in which they give testimony to the world that they have already been converted. The implication of this is twofold. On the one hand, such an understanding of baptism seems to entail a logical distinction between a baptism of the Holy Spirit (conversion) and a baptism with water, which confirms or symbolizes the former. Such a distinction seems biblically founded (see Acts 8:14–17). A second implication of this understanding of baptism would seem to be the insistence upon a believer's baptism to the exclusion of infant baptism. Since on these grounds baptism presupposes faith and conversion, infants are precluded because they are not capable of such experiences.

There seems to be good reason for holding this view. Its biblical foundation is firm insofar as most of the reported baptisms in the New Testament are baptisms of adults. Further, there are indications in some of the Church Fathers that infant baptism was regarded as a novelty rather than part of the biblical tradition.[12] Additionally the case for a believer's baptism seems strengthened when one considers the benefits such a view brings in regards to emphasizing the importance of living the Christian life. This follows from the idea of a believer's baptism, because on these grounds the sacrament has no meaning and effect apart from faith (or the experience of conversion). There is no way baptism can be relegated to a mere mechanistic guarantee of salvation. The medieval idea that the sacrament works and gives grace merely by being celebrated (*ex opere operato*) is completely rejected.

An alternative to this Baptist/Free Church understanding of baptism emerges from among Roman Catholic, Eastern Orthodox, and several Protestant traditions (notably Lutherans and Episcopalians). These traditions believe that baptism does in fact give, not merely symbolize, grace. Baptism is regarded as a "saving event." It transforms those who receive it, making them new creatures. Further, no distinction between water baptism and Spirit baptism can be made. One is transformed in baptism and receives the Holy Spirit. This is fundamentally the orientation of this volume and that of the sermon which will follow.

Representatives of this understanding of baptism have divided somewhat on the question of how this transforming power is related to the recipient's faith. We have already noted the medieval view of *ex opere operato*. According to this view baptism works grace even apart from faith. More typically, however, some necessary role for faith in receiving this grace is asserted. Thus it has been argued by Luther and Augustine, among others, that baptism works grace unconditionally in the recipient but that this grace (transforming power) only benefits the recipient when it is received in faith.[13] On these grounds baptism may be compared to the gift of great athletic ability. One possesses the gift whether one participates in sports or not. However, the gift is only of benefit if the individual practices and develops this ability. (Interestingly enough, some contemporary Roman Catholic theologians are suggesting that this is all *ex opere operato* intends to assert.[14])

Infant baptism is the logical outcome of this view. Infants are to be baptized not just because of original sin. They may be baptized because their inability to have faith, on account of not yet having developed cognitive capacities, does not preclude their receiving the gift of grace in baptism.

As previously noted, biblical foundations for this practice are not impeccable. Jesus' blessing of the little children is often cited as backing for the practice (see Matt. 19:13–15; Mark 10:13–16; Luke 18:15–17). Yet in fact these texts do not refer to baptism at all, but speak only of entering the kingdom. The baptisms of entire households recorded in Acts 16:15, 33 and 1 Corinthians 1:16 have been cited as implying that infants, as members of these households, must have been baptized in biblical times. In fact, however, these texts only suggest that the children of converts may have been baptized. There is no clear New Testament evidence in support of the baptism of children whose parents were already Christian. Ultimately those who advocate infant baptism can make their best appeal to the predominance of the practice throughout the church's history. Surely, it can be argued, God would not allow the church to err for so long if infant baptism were contrary to divine mandate.[15]

The affirmation of infant baptism and the consequent understanding that the sacrament works grace provides a powerful witness to the primacy of God's act in bringing about salvation. This can be a salubrious corrective to tendencies associated with believer's baptism which may imply that salvation is by personal spiritual experience rather than God's objective act.

The Reformed traditions play an interesting mediative role between these two understandings of baptism. On one hand, this tradition practices infant baptism.[16] Yet like the Free Church tradition it does not assert that salvation is accomplished through baptism, but rather through election.[17] As such, baptism is merely a sign or certification of what has already happened and a way of coming to know it. Yet because the baptized one is already elect, it is legitimate to baptize in infancy even though the child has not yet experienced faith. Inasmuch as they have been predestined to faith, infants may be baptized in view of their future faith and because of their place in the covenant community.[18] Thus the Reformed view may offer ecumenical promise of reconciling infant baptism with the symbolic understanding of the sacrament which underlies the believer's baptism view.

It is now possible to conclude this discussion of baptism by raising the question of its significance for daily life. In part this question has already been answered. Baptism entails salvation, a new existence dead to sin and alive with Christ, whether the sacrament be regarded as creating this new reality or merely symbolizing it. In short baptism is correlated with the Christian's new identity. If we recall the meaning of the sacrament's external sign it is evident that this new identity entails a dying to self and rising with Christ (see Rom. 6). As such Christians are self-sacrificing people, daily sacrificing their sinful selves. This is the sense in which we may speak of the priesthood of all believers (see 1 Peter 2:9; Rev. 20:6). All Christians are priests in the sense that all offer sacrifice to God with their lives. Of course such a self-sacrificing lifestyle is not a burden, but a joy. It is a joy because to live such a life is to fulfil one's identity given in baptism. It is a joy in much the same way the great athlete finds joy in the rigors of training.

At this point we begin to consider the question we raised in an earlier chapter about the content of sanctification (Christian life). We can appreciate the content of this lifestyle more fully if we expand a bit more on the meaning of baptism as entrance into the body of Christ.

To belong to Christ is to receive all that he has (be conformed to him). We saw in earlier chapters that this union with Christ is one way of understanding our new identity, justification by grace through faith. In virtue of receiving all that he has, we share in his life, righteousness, salvation, and in his ongoing process of creation. We also share in his death. But our membership in his body entails one more dimension. We share all that belongs to him, including each other (since our brothers and sisters in Christ also belong to him, 1 Cor. 12:12–13). Christians belong to each other in virtue of their baptism. Their new identity is such that they can no longer be themselves without each other.

As a result, Christians are given all sorts of opportunities to be themselves in virtue of belonging to the body of Christ. Because I cannot be myself without bearing all that my neighbor has, membership in the body provides all kinds of opportunities to deny myself for the sake of the neighbor and for the love of God. This is my *vocation* as a Christian, to deny myself for the sake of my neighbor in whatever situation in life I find myself (see Col. 3:23). In such self-denial new good is created, and we come to share in God's ongoing creative process.

All this is given the Christian in baptism. Such a life is made an inextricable part of Christian identity. The following sermon picks up this theme of the difference baptism makes in a person's life. Baptism is important for daily living. It is a reference point for the believer's life, a kind of identity description. It makes us people who are creative on behalf of others. It makes us who we are.

§

Text: Romans 6:2b–11

(*Preached in small, rural congregation.*)

In just a few minutes we will be celebrating a baptism. Of course we all know that baptisms are very important, not only for the family involved but also for the whole church. But do we know why it is so important? What is so special about splashing a baby's forehead three times with water in the name of Father, Son, and Holy Spirit? What is it that is going to happen to Jodi Lynn and to us in just a few minutes?

If we are going to deal with these questions we need to begin with Jesus and his command to baptize believers. "Go therefore and make disciples of all nations, baptizing them in the name of the Father, and of the Son, and of the Holy Spirit," he told his disciples (Matt. 28:19). If we are looking for the reason that we baptize we really need not look elsewhere. If Jesus has instituted this sacrament and commanded us to do it, that should be all the legitimation we need for practicing baptism. Thus in answer to the question of why we are about to have a baptism, our first response can be simple and direct. We baptize because Jesus commanded us to do it.

Of course this observation is only the beginning for our reflections on baptism. We still need to determine God's purpose for having us baptize. This purpose or rationale is probably quite familiar to you. One way of describing the purpose of baptism is that in baptism we become members of the church. That is true. Yet it must be added that in becoming part of the church we also receive salvation. Thus in his letter to Titus, Paul writes: God "saved us, not because of deeds done by us in righteousness, but in virtue of his own mercy, by the washing of regeneration" (Titus 3:5).

Now there is a point of clarification which needs to be made here. It is not the case that baptism is the *cause* of our salvation. Rather, our salvation is brought about by the work of Jesus Christ, through his death and resurrection. In a sense baptism is the *seal* of our salvation. Yet it is more than a mere symbol; it is a kind of telegram.

It is as if a rich, long-lost uncle from Norway died and left me a fortune. This inheritance really does me little good if I know nothing about it. I need something like a telegram to inform me about this fortune my long-lost uncle has left me. Of course the telegram bringing the news of my inheritance is more than a mere symbol of this new found fortune. In a real sense it is a sign which actually brings me the fortune and makes me rich. Yet ultimately the telegram is not the cause of my inheritance; it is the death and loving intention of my uncle which actually causes my fortune to come about.

This is how to understand baptism in relation to the atoning work of Christ. Baptism is really the message or telegram which informs us of God's love for us. In baptism it is proclaimed to everyone, to all of us here, to all Christians, for all time, that God loves this particular child and loves us, too. Thus today through her baptism God is telling us all of love for Jodi Lynn. Yet as with my uncle's telegram, through the administration of this baptism God is also actually giving her love.

This brings us to the question of why God would want us to baptize Jodi now when she is a baby. Why do many segments of the Christian church practice infant baptism rather than postpone the sacrament until children are older and can understand the significance of baptism? The church has typically pointed here to Jesus' remark to the disciples: "Let the children come to me, do not hinder them; for to such belongs the kingdom of God" (Mark 10:14; also see Matt. 19:14 and Luke 18:16). Perhaps its best argument, though, is to appeal to the church's historic practice of baptizing infants. One would certainly not expect God to have allowed an incorrect practice to persist for so great a length of time.[19] Nevertheless, there is yet one more consideration which mandates the baptism of infants. It is a practice which unambiguously affirms that God is the author of our salvation.

Recall my notion of baptism as God's message to us about our salvation. Salvation and God's love cannot be earned. They are entirely God's gift. There are no preconditions or requirements necessary in order to receive God's love. In this respect we are completely helpless, fully dependent on God's mercy. What could be more helpless than a little baby, so completely dependent on everything and everyone? That is precisely the point of infant baptism. As we sit in our pews this morning and participate in Jodi Lynn's baptism, we are reminded that when it comes to attaining salvation we are all just as helpless as she. As Jodi herself grows up and asks her parents about her baptism they will be able to tell her that before she was aware of anything, before she could talk or think or understand, she already had received God's love and the promise of salvation. It is the same with us. Of course it is certainly not the case that those of us who were baptized later in life have lost out on this. Yet the reason many segments of the church encourage the baptism of children is to emphasize to all of us that salvation is *totally* the work of God and not our own.

It will be helpful to summarize what we have learned so far. We have seen that in baptism we receive the message of our salvation. Also we have come to understand that the baptism of infants serves to underline the fact that this salvation we receive is totally God's work and that there is nothing we can do to earn it. However there is yet one more thing about baptism that we need to consider if we are to understand it properly. Quite honestly, what I want to talk about now is something that I'm afraid most Christians do not fully appreciate. You see, usually when we think about baptism, we tend to think of it as a once-and-done event. In some ways that is true; once we are baptized we never need to be baptized again. But did you know that your entire life as a Christian is one long baptism, that we live our whole lives under the sign of baptism?

In the sixth chapter of Romans, the Apostle Paul deals with this whole issue. He writes:

> Do you not know that all of us who have been baptized into Christ Jesus were baptized into his death? We were buried therefore with him by baptism into death, so that as Christ was raised from the dead by the glory of the Father, we too might walk in newness of life.
>
> For if we have been united with him in a death like his, we shall certainly be united with him in a resurrection like his. We know that our old self was crucified with him. . . . So you also must consider yourselves dead to sin and alive to God in Christ Jesus. (Rom. 6:3–6, 11)

In baptism we died to sin and are now alive to Jesus Christ. In fact, there is a certain symbolism in the baptism service which indicates that we have indeed died to sin. In a few minutes I will take Jodi Lynn in my hands and immerse her in water. As the water covers her it is as though she is drowning; that is, her old sinful self, the self that would rebel against God, is being put to death. Of course I know it sounds funny to talk about a little baby being sinful. After all, what has she done wrong? Yet if we remember that sin can also be understood as selfishness, as the concern with oneself to the exclusion of everyone else, then we have to admit that even little babies are tinged with sin. This is the deeper truth we find in the Genesis story, that all of us, everyone of us has sinned and fallen short of the glory of God.

If it is true that even a baby is stained with selfishness and sin, then that sinful part of her must to put to death. As we have already said, this is what happened to us when we were immersed in the baptismal waters. That in us which is sinful died. This happened because we were linked to Christ's death on the cross and joined to his body. The old being, that in us which was marred by sin, is now dead. Subsequently, though, we were and Jodi will be withdrawn from the water. That signifies the resurrection which we now share with Christ. God's Word working through the baptismal waters has drowned us and killed our old sinful selves, but now we have arisen out of these waters as new people.

We are people whose new identity has been shaped by our membership in Christ's body. (Our baptism has brought about our initiation into this body.) As such as have been made people who are dead to sin, who share all that belongs to Christ. His righteousness, his salvation, his creative activities, and all the members of his body belong to us. So our baptisms have made us people who have the promise of salvation, people who share in God's creative projects, and people who belong to each other. This is our identity. The real me is a person who identifies with God's work, who sacrifices himself (dies to sin) on behalf of the neighbor who is inextricably linked with me. I cannot be myself without my neighbor. Thus I cannot be myself if I yield to sin and put my own before my neighbor's welfare. The real me is a person who sacrifices himself, who dies to sin on behalf of his neighbor for the sake of Christ's creative projects. Baptism provides us with a kind of Christ-like identity.

I need to make some qualifications at this point. Important distinctions must be made between Christ and the new identity given us in baptism. Unlike Christ, our dying to sin in our neighbors' service does not bring their salvation. Also it needs to be noted that unlike Christ, even though we have died to sin in baptism, even though our old sinful selves have been drowned, there is no doubt that all of us are still sinners. There are no perfect people sitting here among us in this sanctuary. At least I don't know any, and that certainly includes myself. Does that mean our baptisms did not work? Should we all go back to the baptismal font and do it again properly? No, that is not the problem at all. Baptism is only a beginning. In the event of baptism we receive the promise that in the end our sinful side will be beaten back. Yet it is still the case that sin remains; on this side of death there is no such thing as perfection. Thus our baptisms simply begin a lifelong process of dying to our sinful selves so that we can truly share in God's creative projects. The new self-sacrificing identity we have been given in baptism is a bit like the gift of great athletic or musical ability. Our identity is defined by these abilities, and they can never be taken away from us. Yet they are not fully developed apart from practice. As musicians require a great deal of practice to fulfil their musical promise, so Christians practice denying themselves on behalf of the neighbor to fulfil the promise of their baptism. It is in this sense that our whole lives should be a living out of our baptism. In every event of life we are called to renew our baptismal vows. Yet this call to renewal is not a burden; it is a joy for those who have been baptized. Back to my analogy: people who are musical must practice, yet because they love music (have it in their blood), they love to practice. So we Christians find joy in serving our neighbor because Christ's new life is in our blood.

Perhaps now you can see why baptism is so important, not just for the family involved, but for all of us. With Jodi Lynn's baptism today we are being asked a question that we will spend the rest of our lives answering. Will you allow your sinful self to be drowned, denying it daily for Christ's sake on behalf of your neighbor? Baptism comes at the beginning of life because it sets the tone for all the rest; it is something we need to renew, a question we need to answer again and again.

Of course one more consideration must be added. The question posed by our baptism ultimately already has an answer. And the answer is that the love of God, God's overwhelming love, is for us. That is what makes baptism so important. It puts a mark on us, makes us self-sacrificing people loved by God, even if we fail to practice it in our lives. Baptism makes us persons who, like Jodi, will live in that love every day of our lives. Go and do likewise, my friends. Amen.

Chapter Thirteen

THE LORD's SUPPER

The Lord's Supper is the second rite whose sacramental status is ecumenically recognized. It is sometimes called the eucharist (εὐχαριαστία), which literally means thanksgiving. Other times the sacrament is called Holy Communion. This connotes its character as a common meal shared by a community. The implications of designating the Lord's Supper by both of these terms will subsequently warrant attention.

Of course the sacrament was instituted by Jesus on the evening before his death (Matt. 26:17–29; Mark 14:12–16; Luke 22:7–13). On that evening Jesus gathered his disciples together to eat a meal. It was an important occasion for several reasons. The meal was a celebration of the Jewish Seder. The Seder commemorates the Hebrews' escape from Egypt under Moses. The meal includes unleavened bread and wine, the very elements used by Jesus (see Deut. 16:1–8). The Lord's Supper has its roots in an ancient festival which celebrates freedom. Therefore the freedom given in Christ (John 8:36) and received in this sacrament is a fulfillment of Old Testament promises.

The Last Supper was also a monumental occasion for Jesus and his followers precisely because it was the final meal they would eat together before the Passion. This was a particular landmark in view of the significant role many scholars believe table fellowship played in cementing the relationship between Jesus and his followers. In fact it has been suggested that the Lord's Supper played such a central role in the early church because it afforded the disciples an opportunity to reflect on the fond memories of the meals they had shared with Jesus.[1] This focus on table fellowship is also evident insofar as the early church celebrated the Lord's Supper as a common meal rather than as a special rite or worship service (1 Cor. 11:20–21; Jude 12). Since the practice was only discontinued because of certain abuses peculiar to the early church, it may be that contemporary Christians should reassess the significance of the meal-character of this sacrament.

All of us recognize what a central part the elements of bread and wine play in the Lord's Supper. Understanding their status provides insights about what existential benefits the sacrament offers. All Christians agree that some way there is a close correlation between Jesus and the elements. "This is my body" (Matt. 26:26.): to receive the elements is to receive Christ. As with baptism and justification, to receive him is to receive all he has. It follows, then, that the sacrament gives forgiveness of sins (Matt. 26:28). It does not convey this gift because of some magical quality of the sacramental elements. It only gives these gifts because Christ is so intimately related to the sacramental event.

All Christians can agree on these issues. Disagreements begin to emerge when we consider how to speak of the relationship between Christ and the sacramental elements. Four different views have appeared in the history of the church.

The traditional Roman Catholic position is called *transubstantiation*. The intention of this position is to affirm that Christ is really present in the elements. The argument is that the words of institution, when pronounced by a duly-ordained priest, transform the elements into the body and blood of Christ. The elements are no longer bread and wine; their substance has been changed, *trans*formed, into Christ's body and blood. The elements may still look like bread and wine, yet that is just an accident. The new substance created in the consecration is really, substantially Christ's body and blood. The words of institution transform the elements in this way regardless of the faith of the recipient. Even unbelievers receive Christ in the sacrament. Thus the sacrament works by working (*ex opere operato*).[2]

Contemporary Roman Catholics have reinterpreted this dogma, and on the basis of this reinterpretation they have moved closer to the Lutheran position which will be described below. Thus evaluation of transubstantiation would be premature.

Another, and opposite, position on the status of the elements is the symbolic view of sixteenth-century Reformer Ulrich Zwingli. (This view predominates in most of Protestantism.) His position is that the elements merely symbolize Christ's body and blood. They make us think of Jesus, remember him. Christ is not actually present in the elements.[3]

The prime advantage of this view is obvious. It is more intellectually credible. The elements look like bread and wine; thus they should be deemed bread and wine. Furthermore, this view is advantageous in providing an emphasis on the role of faith in the sacrament. On its grounds the recipient benefits nothing from the sacrament apart from faith. Since Christ is not really present the sole benefit of the sacrament is remembering him. This necessitates faith.

Questions have been raised about the Zwinglian view. One concern is that the emphasis on faith may compromsise the objectivity of grace which characterizes a real-presence view. (Grace is objective in the Roman Catholic tradition in the sense that grace is present regardless of the believer's response. In that sense a better witness to justification by grace is given.) A second problematic issue is the difficulty this view has in accounting for the actual New Testament witness concerning the Supper. "This is my body" (Matt. 26:26). One needs to read this text in light of certain prior exegetical commitments in order to conclude that Jesus intended a strictly symbolic presence in the sacrament.

The theology of John Calvin provides a kind of mediating position between the first two proposals. Unlike Zwingli, practitioners of this view insist that Christ is really present. In the sacrament we actually receive Christ and his benefits, not just a memory or a symbol. This is one of the strengths of this view.

Unlike the Roman Catholic and Lutheran positions, though, Calvin did not believe that Christ is present physically in the elements. In this regard his position shares some of the rational credibility associated with the symbolic view. How then is Christ present in the Supper if he is not in the elements? The image Calvin uses to describe his presence is that of the "heavenly ascent." The elements provide us with access to ascent to heaven where the heavenly Christ is present to us. An emphasis on the recipient's faith, characteristic of the symbolic view, is also inherent in Calvin's mediating proposal. Given his view, one does not ascend to Christ's presence apart from faith. Because Christ is not present in the elements without faith, the unbelieving recipient receives mere bread and wine.[4]

The Lutheran view is another mediating position. It is much in agreement with Calvin. Luther insisted that Christ is really present and yet that the elements remain bread and wine. However, unlike Calvin, Lutherans believe that the elements are not mere bread and wine. Christ is really present *in* them.[5]

This commitment places the Lutheran position in an apparent logical fallacy. How can an element be *both* bread and Christ's body at the same time? Fundamentally Lutherans appeal to mystery at this point. Yet their position has often been accused of certain unintended misconceptions. In popular piety the insistence on the bread and wine character of the elements has led some laity to regard the Lutheran position as a symbolic view of the sacrament. Others have claimed incorrectly that Lutherans taught a position of *consubstantiation*. Consubstantiation was a medieval heresy which argued that when consecrated the elements became a hybrid substance, a synthesis of Christ's body and bread. Lutherans, by contrast, intend to affirm that the consecrated elements are *both* ordinary bread and Christ's body at the same time. The problem is how to describe this. How can an element or event be two things at once?

The problem of dealing with this question in a credible fashion has been a difficult one for this approach. I am convinced, though, that we can overcome this objection. Without negating the concrete reality of the events, love is really present in the embrace of devoted husband and wife or in busy parents bringing a baseball-loving child to a game. In the same way Christ can be present in bread and wine without negating their qualities as real bread and wine. The

Christological analogy is also helpful at this point in rendering the position intelligible. As the person of Christ can be both divine and human without confusion of the natures, so the sacramental element can be both bread and Christ's body without confusion.

To the degree that these reflections have rendered the Lutheran position more intelligible we should assess its strengths. The analogy between the incarnation and the real presence of Christ in the elements is a powerful one. Unlike other proposals considered, this position truly attests to the incarnation. As God became human by joining human flesh in the incarnation, so Christ comes to humanity by joining himself to earthly elements (rather than our ascending to him or reflecting on him). The incarnation is God's movement "downward" to us. This is the logical direction of the Lutheran view of the real presence of Christ in the Lord's Supper.

A second strength of this view is its ability to affirm both the objectivity of grace and the importance of faith. Lutherans believe that Christ is really present regardless of one's faith. Yet they agree with Calvin and Zwingli in insisting that the sacrament is not beneficial without faith. The unbeliever receives Christ, but Christ is received to the recipient's judgment, not benefit (as law, not as gospel).

Finally this position possesses a third strength which warrants consideration. Its mediating position between transubstantiation and the symbolic view offers hope for ecumenical rapprochement. This has already begun to be realized, inasmuch as contemporary Roman Catholic theologians have found themselves in substantial agreement with the Lutheran position. In their view Transubstantiation should not be regarded as a literal explanation of Christ's real presence in the sacrament. Rather the dogma is only intended to assert the real presence.[6] Presumably the issue of whether the elements remain bread and wine or are totally transformed is not deemed a central matter. For this reason the Lutheran position, which holds that the elements remain bread and wine and yet affirms with equal vigor (as do the Catholics) that Christ is really present, is acceptable from a Roman Catholic viewpoint. Lest anyone regard this rapprochement as the product of a fundamental change in contemporary Roman Catholic thinking, it should be noted that the great medieval Catholic theologian, Thomas Aquinas, held that the main rationale for transubstantiation was to affirm the real presence.[7]

In view of these Lutheran-Catholic agreements, the great degree of convergence between Calvinism and Lutheranism and the fact that all three would be able to accept the Zwinglian contention that the elements do not lose their status as bread and wine, ecumenical agreement on the question of the status of the elements seems to be a growing possibility.[8] At least Christians can begin to ask whether their disagreements are so significant that they should preclude table fellowship.

There is a second area of disagreement among Christians about the Lord's Supper which is also moving toward ecumenical rapprochement. This is the issue of whether the Lord's Supper (the Mass) is a sacrifice. It was one of the issues which precipitated the Reformation. The sixteenth-century Reformers thought that Roman Catholics were teaching that the Mass is a *propitiatory* sacrifice. A propitiatory sacrifice would mean that the Mass is a work of satisfaction which placates God's wrath. Were that the case, a denial of the sufficiency of Christ's redeeming work would have been implied. His sacrifice would be seen as insufficient, requiring additional sacrifices in order to complete it. This is clearly an unsatisfactory proposal. It undercuts the Christian commitment to the fact that salvation is through Christ alone (*sola Christi*), and it implies that humans redeem themselves by offering sacrifices to God.

Contemporary scholarship has shown that this is not the Roman Catholic position. Thus Thomas Aquinas spoke of the Mass as sacrifice in the sense that it represents the one true sacrifice (i.e., Christ) and that through it the work of redemption is carried on in us.[9] Protestants, it would seem, could support this view. All would affirm that in some sense the Lord's Supper represents Christ. The idea that because the sacrament carries on the work of redemption in us it may be called a sacrifice is quite intelligible in light of our reflections in the last chapter on the impact of baptism. We noted at that time that one aspect of the identity given us in baptism is that the baptized are made self-sacrificing people. They sacrifice their sinful selves for the sake of Christ and the neighbor. To the degree that the eucharist nurtures this sacrificial lifestyle it may properly be deemed a sacrifice.

This notion has venerable roots in Protestantism. Luther was willing to deem the Mass a sacrifice as long as it was clear that it is believers who are sacrificed in the sacrament.[10] We are sacrificed in the sense that the sacrament nurtures our inclination to deny and sacrifice ourselves. There seems to be no reason why any Christian body could not accept the notion of the eucharist as a sacrifice on these grounds. Additionally it is common for several Protestant bodies to speak of eucharistic sacrifices (sacrifices of praise and thanksgiving).[11] The Lord's Supper may be called a sacrifice in this sense inasmuch as participants offer sacrifices of praise. The idea of the eucharist as sacrifice seems on these grounds to be no barrier to table fellowship among Christians.

These reflections bear upon the question of the significance of the Lord's Supper for our daily lives. The previous chapter on baptism has already provided some insights about the impact of the sacraments on believers. Through baptism God makes people part of the body of Christ and gives them their identity as self-sacrificing, creative people. This is nurtured by other sacraments. The physical dimension of the sacraments is significant, particularly in regard to the Lord's Supper. In baptism and justification the Christian is united with Christ. This union is nurtured in all sorts of ways (preaching, prayer, fellowship with others, service). Yet no more intense union could be envisioned than in the Lord's Supper where the believer receives Christ by faith through the mouth. The significance of the sacrament, then, is that believers participate in total union with Christ, as intimate as the union between me and the food I ate at breakfast this morning. The Lord's Supper makes my relationship with Christ more intimate.

The sacrament also has other dimensions which are relevant to our lives. These are evident in the alternate designations used to describe the sacrament. We have noted that the Lord's Supper may also be called the eucharist, meaning thanksgiving. In view of the opportunity it provides for intensifying our relationship with Christ (by receiving him through the mouth), this sacrament should be an occasion for thanksgiving and praise. Unfortunately this theme is reflected too seldom in our actual worship practices. Often the Lord's Supper is celebrated in a somber, joyless atmosphere. Christians need to consider how best to introduce the elements of genuine celebration, thanksgiving, and joy into the Lord's Supper.

The sacrament is also termed Holy Communion, in reference to its communal aspect (its work in building the body of Christ). It does this insofar as we receive Christ's body. To receive Christ is to receive all that belongs to him, including other believers who belong to him. As much as Christ, these other believers become a part of my new identity, such that I cannot be myself apart from them. It is in this sense that the Lord's Supper builds community.

As with the element of thanksgiving and praise, contemporary Christian worship practices have not done a satisfactory job in witnessing to the communal dimension of the Sacrament. The following sermon speaks to this issue. The presupposition is that the sacrament imparts objective grace. It has had the impact of shaping a sense of community in the church even if we did not recognize it as such. That is the way God sometimes works. One relevant dimension of the Lord's Supper for us is that it is nurturing our common identity, making us people with common hopes and goals who can and want to work together to glorify God.

§

Text: 1 Corinthians 10:14–17; 12:4–12
(*Preached in seminary chapel.*)

You know, one of the nice things about being a newcomer in a community is that everyone is interested in your opinion. The questions never end it seems. "How do you like it here? What do you think of this place and us? Is it like you expected it to be?" Yes, when you are a newcomer those questions keep popping up in conversations. And since Betsey and I have arrived in this community we have had plenty of opportunities to say what we think of the community.

In trying to express what makes this place so special, many images run across my mind. Some evenings ago as I sat down to prepare this sermon, I was struck by that hymn of Christian unity found in 1 Corinthians 12. That is it, I thought! It is the commonality of this place that is striking. People here share so much together. That is what strikes me about this and other Christian communities to which I have belonged. Our commonality is so evident. You can sense it as you talk to others and find that their hopes and dreams are kind of like your own. There is a sense of having shared the same experiences, values, and even fears. And I ask myself, what is the source of that commonality?

I began to think: could it be because we are mostly all middle-class American Christians? Well, to some extent maybe, but in reality there are social and economic differences among us. As for doctrinal unanimity, you can forget that. There is too much theological diversity in this community to think doctrine binds us together. What about our common vocational interests? Perhaps that is what cements our unanimity. Yet when you get a bunch of doctors, lawyers, or other professional people together, you really find very little that unifies them. So I sat there at my desk that evening, thinking about what could be the source of the commonality I have experienced in this place. I thought about the thing we do many times when we gather together: celebrate the eucharist. I wondered: could it be that our commonality is ultimately rooted in the simple fact that we have eaten a few of these eucharist meals together?

I suspect that my proposal, locating the source of the church's unity in the eucharistic meal, is not very startling. It is something theologians are supposed to say in conjunction with the Lord's Supper, to talk about the body of Christ and all that. Yet the meal character of the eucharist and the image of table fellowship correlated with it are very compelling images. Think about them with me for a moment now, and let us see if they do not speak a very concrete, realistic word about the commonality that is among us.

For me, you see, the image of table fellowship communicates alot. I come out of a strong Scandinavian background and have certain elements of an old-world upbringing. One of the areas where that came out loud and clear was in the family attitude toward mealtime.

For the Ellingsen family I think mealtime might have been the most important time of the day. It was always a time for sharing the day's events, a time for good talk. Sometimes it could get pretty raucous, especially when extended family got in the act. Yelling and arguing, with a couple of hugs thrown in too, but it was us; it was real; it was a time really to be ourselves.

I think of mealtimes, and I have other memories. I think of my parents telling me how the family table was reserved for people you love. The stories they tell of how you really knew you had it made with my grandfather if he invited you home for a meal. It was the highest compliment he and my grandmother could pay. And I think of my mother looking testily at someone who had stabbed another friend in the back and saying: "I wouldn't break bread with that woman if she had the last piece of bread on earth." Mealtime is a time for people you love.

Then I think of the present. I think of mealtimes that Betsey and I share. It very often seems that we talk just a little more and a little more deeply over a good steak or roast. Betsey and I also love to remember meals we have shared with good friends. We treasure all the joys we have shared with those dear friends over many happy meals—the good conversation, the kinship, the fellowship. Mealtime is when you can really get to know somebody.

It is not just the Ellingsens, family and friends, who have this kind of kinship with the sharing of a common meal. It is a universal experience, but perhaps it was even more prevalent in ancient cultures. Therefore, it is not outlandish to suspect that table fellowship was similarly valued by Jesus and his friends as well.

In saying this I provide no new insight about the New Testament. Many scholars have noticed the role table fellowship played in Jesus' relationship with the twelve (see Matt. 9:15; Mark 2:16; Luke 14). And it makes sense, doesn't it? Just think of all the various meals that are reported in the Gospels involving Jesus and the disciples. Unlike other religionists of their day, the disciples do not fast while Jesus is among them. Jesus *eats* with the sinners and Pharisees. And when he teaches, think how often the images of the wedding banquet and the feast appear (see Matt. 22:1–4; Luke 14:16–24). Think of the miracles: he *feeds* the four and five thousand (Mark 6:30–44; 8:1–10; Luke 9:10–17). Table fellowship with Jesus seems to have had a very important place in the New Testament church. For the disciples it may have been the time when Jesus made his deepest impression on them.

And then there was the Last Supper. Jesus and his disciples gather for the final breaking of bread together. They had shared much at mealtime. I think of it in terms of the fellowship my family, friends, and I have shared at meals. Now all that seemed to be ending. Until Jesus proceeded to promise the disciples that henceforth he would be present to them when they shared bread and wine in this very special kind of meal.

It hits home, doesn't it? The real presence: Jesus is really present in the sacrament in the same way that he was present in sharing table fellowship with the twelve. And though I had not really appreciated it until recently, a "personalistic" understanding of Christ's presence in the eucharist is a very legitimate position. Jesus is really present in the sense that he is personally available for fellowship with us at this common meal. The church's unity, the commonality we share in this community, is after all grounded in this common meal.

If you don't believe me, 1 Corinthians 10—12 may convince you. It is quite evident that all three chapters belong together as a piece. The problem that concerned Paul throughout this portion of the letter was the disunity of the Corinthian church. That disunity was, among other places, manifesting itself in the way the Lord's Supper was practiced. About that Paul wrote: "The bread which we break, is it not a participation in the body of Christ? Because there is one loaf, we who are many are one body, for we all partake of the same loaf" (1 Cor. 10:16–17).

The crucial words here are "participate" and "partake." The Greek word in both cases is "κοινωνία" fellowship. So literally Paul is saying here that we have fellowship in the body of Christ through the bread we break. Then he goes on to discuss the nature of our unity in the body in chapter twelve. The unity we share in the church, our commonality, is quite evidently connected with the fellowship we share with Christ and with each other in this common meal.

Let's penetrate this a bit more. It is not hard now to see how our commonality is nurtured this way—not hard now that we know what goes on at a meal. It is not hard to figure out why despite our diverse paths we in this community have so much in common. It is due to the fact that for lo these many years, even though our paths have not crossed, we have shared table fellowship at a meal like this with a common host. After all, he seems to have promised the twelve to be personally present, and as in any good meal we have shared our real selves with our host and he has shared himself with us.

No wonder Christians have so much in common. We have had a common eating partner, whose presence obviously influences us to share common interests, common goals, and common experiences. That usually results from good table fellowship, a kind of mutual influencing, a genuine sharing. Even more than that, inasmuch as our host is present whenever this special meal is celebrated even if it happens in different locations, it seems to follow that in some hidden way we have all been sharing table fellowship together with our common host at his table. No wonder we share so much in common. We have broken bread together and been sharing the fellowship and common influences that go with it our entire lives.

Come and eat, friends. It is easy to see how the meal character of this sacrament upholds and supports the church's unity. Strengthening our unity, the fellowship that God established among us in our baptism, is what the Lord's Supper is all about. Meals like this have a way of bringing people closer together, in this case closer to our host (making us more Christlike). As the Ellingsens would say: "The family that eats together stays and loves together." Enjoy the fellowship, friends, and celebrate it. Amen.

Chapter Fourteen

ESCHATOLOGY AND THE RESURRECTION OF THE BODY

The doctrine of eschatology is concerned with the "last things." Eschatology refers to matters related to Christ's second coming, when the kingdom of God will be fully realized. Questions about the status of humans after death also belong to the doctrine of eschatology.

Some New Testament scholars have argued that eschatology was the heart of the early church's message. It is certainly true that Jesus proclaimed an eschatological message ("Repent, for the kingdom of heaven is at hand" Matt. 4:17). On the basis of his preaching, his earliest followers may have expected the imminent *parousia*, that is, Christ's immediate second coming. When he did not return immediately it became necessary to establish institutions and ceremonies which would keep this hope alive. The church always understood itself as an eschatological community. However, given this reconstruction of the history of the early church, all dimensions of the Christian life, including the sacraments, spiritual gifts, and the like must be deemed as conveying the eschatological expectation.[1]

These insights pose a challenge to the contemporary church. We have tended to think about eschatology solely in terms of *future eschatology*. The eschaton/parousia is something that will happen someday. Rather we need to consider more seriously the sense in which the eschaton has already been realized. Such a *realized eschatology* would then be truer to the New Testament witness. It would also have practical consequences for the life of the church.

Unquestionably, more emphasis on a realized eschatology and on how the church, the sacraments, and other dimensions of faith point to the eschaton would restore a sense of urgency and expectation to the church's work. It is quite likely that Paul and other missionaries of the early church were so diligent in their tasks because their eschatological expectations that Christ would come soon made them feel a sense of urgency. In a time like ours when the church too often postpones its mandates and waits to marshal resources, this eschatological sense would be a healthy corrective. Finally, Jesus' message of the coming kingdom was a word of hope. Given the hopelessness of our narcissistic society, the eschatological Word which proclaims that "now" is the moment when God is creating anew is important and relevant. (This will be illustrated by the sermon included in this chapter.) The church has been too inclined to abandon eschatological concerns to sectarian and cult mentalities.

In that connection the eschatological aberrations which orthodox Christianity rejects should be considered briefly. Christians do not necessarily hold an apocalyptic vision of reality. To be *apocalyptic* is to believe that Christ's second coming is imminent. It often manifests itself in predictions about the date of the parousia. Jesus would have believers to be always ready (realized eschatology), but he seems to discourage our ability to predict the time when the kingdom will come (Matt. 24:42; cf. 1 Thess. 5:2).

In like manner most Christian communities reject *chiliasm* and *millennialism*. These views refer to a period of one thousand years in which Christ will reign prior to the end of the world. These beliefs are founded on a literal reading of Revelation 20. Apart from exegetical questions about reading a text from Revelation literally (since the book is more like poetry), the problem with this view is that it tends to manifest itself in a belief that the faithful will be rewarded with material blessings. These views undercut the doctrine of justification by grace apart from works of the law. They do so by setting up a kind of merit system, a system of rewards for believers.

Since Christians encounter many sectarian groups who hold these views it is important that the contemporary church have something to say about eschatology in addition to disagreeing with these views. Reappropriating what can be said constructively about realized eschatology (the sense in that each moment is full of hope and urgency) is absolutely essential for an effective contemporary witness.

Of course future eschatology, particularly the question of what happens in death, is an issue which also must be considered at this point. In order to make this concept meaningful to the modern world, contemporary Christians must work hard to provide concrete images for describing eternal life. In so doing perhaps we can establish more awareness of how the eschatological vision is relevant for us today in appreciating our bodies and our God-given identities, which the concept of a bodily resurrection affirms. There is much at stake in clarifying the concept because the eschatological message (like the doctrine of justification) has an impact/influence on all dimensions of Christian faith, including an unconditional affirmation of who we are.

One presupposition of the preceding remarks is a rejection of *purgatory*. The concept of purgatory is accepted by Roman Catholics as a halfway point between heaven and hell where believers are purged of sin before being made fit to enter heaven. However, this idea does not seem to have biblical support and seems to trade on a body-soul dualism while suggesting a legalist system of making recompense to God. (This is not to say that the idea actually compromises the doctrine of justification by grace. Yet justification is only affirmed adequately to the extent that it is related to the Roman Catholic-scholastic view of justification. This view holds that justification is not complete apart from the full remission of sins. Thus the Christian requires a time of further purification from sin in order to complete the process of justification. This opportunity for purification is provided by purgatory.)

In this connection the question is inevitably raised concerning whom this resurrection of the body is for. The chapter on the atonement has already suggested this. We learned that universal salvation cannot be affirmed unambiguously on biblical grounds. However, if one takes an "actuality" position on what the atonement accomplishes,[2] one may be open to the hope articulated by Karl Barth that "in the reality of God and man in Jesus Christ there is contained much more than we might expect and therefore the supremely unexpected withdrawal of that final threat, i.e., that in the truth of this reality there might be contained the super-abundant promise of the final deliverance of all."[3] At least we may say that God wills that the vision of life given us by Christ be shared with all (1 Tim. 2:4; 2 Cor. 5:19).

This vision of the resurrected life does not and should not have the final word on eschatology. We have already noted the early church's expectation of an imminent in-breaking of the kingdom, and the implications of this for maintaining a realized eschatology. This appreciation that the kingdom has been realized or will be realized in the present moment implies hope and urgency for contemporary Christians. It implies hope in a hopeless world because realized eschatology conveys the message that a new day has come. It also implies urgency because realized eschatology means that *now* is the moment when God comes, and we need to be ready to meet God or we might miss the kingdom.

There are indeed important insights for both parish and personal life in an appreciation of realized eschatology. The church needs to come to a new awareness of these dimensions. The following sermon endeavors to provide an awareness of what it means in our life together to have a God whose kingdom is coming in each new moment and who is always pointing us to the future.

§

Text: Mark 1:29–39
(*Preached in blue-collar congregation.*)

The little town of Capernaum was buzzing. News about the stranger and what he had done on that Sabbath day was spreading like wildfire. Those of you who were here last Sunday already know in part what had happened. First, Jesus had gone into the local synagogue to preach and discuss the Bible with the rabbis. His knowledge of Scripture and the authority with which he taught had simply amazed everyone there that morning. Then on top of that he had healed or at least quieted down a crazy man. That was not all Jesus had done on that Sabbath day. Immediately after the service he had left the synagogue and entered the house of Simon Peter, one of his disciples. (Apparently Peter was from Capernaum.) Jesus was not there long before Peter told him that his mother-in-law was very sick. Obviously, Peter was hinting to Jesus that he just might try his hand at another healing, and before anyone in the house knew what happened Peter's mother-in-law was up and about taking care of everyone's needs (Mark 1:21–31).

As I noted, you could not keep news like that quiet in a town the size of Capernaum. Thus by evening there was a whole flock of people at Peter's house hoping Jesus would heal them, too. And sure enough, he did (Mark 1:32–34). By now Jesus had it made in Capernaum; he could have been elected king if he had wanted it. It is quite likely that this kind of praise and acclaim was something Jesus was not used to. Suddenly he had all the fame and attention anyone could possibly want.

At any rate, the next day Jesus went out to a lonely place a mile or so from town to pray. After awhile Peter and some of the other disciples found him. "Every one is searching for you," Peter said, as if to hint that Jesus really ought to come back to town and enjoy all the attention he was getting. Why not? After all, Jesus really had earned all the praise, and on top of that, things were kind of nice for his followers back there, too. Being close to the center of attention also made them pretty important. It was probably kind of exciting for Peter and the other disciples to be "big shots." Then Jesus dropped the bombshell on them: "Let us go to the next towns, that I may preach there also, for that is why I came out." Jesus actually was willing to give up all the acclaim and the fame to go out and try something new, and that is exactly what he did (Mark 1:35–39).

What does all of this have to do with us? Can Jesus' decision to leave Capernaum in favor of going to preach in other cities and towns possibly be relevant to us in the decisions we make? That depends on what you understand to be involved in a decision. I think a great number of the decisions we make involve a choice between doing things the way we have always done them or changing things for the better. And usually, the way things have always been is not that satisfactory.

Let me show you what I mean by pointing to our story. Jesus had spent some time in Capernaum, and as I have already mentioned, things were quite comfortable. There was every reason to stay there and, seemingly, very little reason to move on. Yet move on Jesus did. A very good question to ask here would be "Why?" Who in their right mind would leave a situation where they were well-known, respected, and comfortable for who-knows-what? I certainly would not want to, would you? But you know, Jesus was like that; he was a man of action who was rarely content to sit around accepting the way things were. Think about it for a minute. When you think of Jesus, don't you almost always think of him on the go? He moved from one miracle to another, from one crowd to another, from one town to another, always preaching, teaching, or healing. In fact, if you take note in your Bibles, the very first word of our Gospel lesson is "immediately." According to Mark, Jesus was always doing things *immediately* (εὐθύς)—right away.

Since Jesus reveals who God is, Jesus' activity must also tell us something about what God is like. Thus in Jesus we learn that God is also always on the go, never content with the way things are. The very act of creation itself represents a change on God's part from the way things were before the creation. God's decision to send the Son to earth to die for us was a change from the way God was relating to us before Jesus came. It was a new way of creating. God, you see, is always willing to change and create anew in order to make things better.

This means that God oftentimes calls us to change, to do something new. To be part of Christ's body is to be a participant in God's ongoing work of creating new good. There are great examples in the history of God's people that show this. Abraham was perfectly happy in the land of Haran, but God told him and Sarah to leave there and go to a new land. Slavery wasn't any bowl of cherries for the people of Israel, but at least they knew what to expect. Yet they followed Moses into the wilderness because they knew that was what God wanted for them. The disciples, men like

Peter, were perfectly happy being fishermen until one day Jesus appeared and told them to give up what they had and follow him. That is what is entailed by being a disciple, you see, a willingness to change.

The applicability of all this to our parish is quite evident. There are times when, like every Christian congregation, we get too comfortable with the way things have always been done. We get so comfortable with our traditions that we become unwilling even to consider change. The fallacy of such an attitude is all too apparent. We see it in the apathy and loss of excitement which can ensue when things become too stagnant. Today we see the fallacy of such an attitude through our text. We learn that not to be open to change is contrary to the spirit of Christian faith. It would be as if Jesus had decided to stay in Capernaum and enjoy all the fame, even though he knew God had other plans for him. Or it would be as if Abraham had said: "No thank you, God. I know it's a good offer you're making me if I'll follow you, but I really don't want to leave my home here in Haran."

It is evident that our God is a God of the future—a God who is declaring that *now* is the time when things are being made new. Jesus' preaching reflects this theme. What else is his call, to believe for the kingdom is at hand, but a declaration that God is about to create anew (see Matt. 4:17; Mark 1:15)? The earliest Christians also fervently held this belief in the urgency of their work, for God's kingdom was at hand (1 Peter 4:7; cf. Acts 2:17). They believed the end times, the eschaton, would soon come. Of course this sense that the end times have come, that at this time God is bringing in the kingdom, does not imply that all we now possess and hold dear belongs to the old order and so must be rejected. On the contrary, tradition and heritage are God's good gifts to us, and we should cherish them. Yet to appreciate that the future which God is creating is already present does imply that if we refuse to be open to change we may miss the moment. God may be passing us by. That is our gospel lesson's message for us today.

One final word: to this point we have been reflecting on the urgency that comes with the realization that this is the time of God's eschaton for our life together in this parish. This morning's lesson (and the doctrine of eschatology) also applies to our own personal lives.

So many of us, even some of us right here, get locked into situations with which we are really unhappy, yet we are afraid to change. Maybe it involves living in a town or in an area which we really do not like; maybe it is being locked into an uncomfortable family situation with parents, or into certain unhappy patterns of relating as husband and wife. No matter what it is, one thing is certain: to refuse to make changes is to refuse to hear God's call. Even if we are unhappy in our present circumstances, the present is always comfortable because we know what to expect. To make changes can be very uncomfortable, because to change is to face the unknown. God keeps on calling us, just as with Jesus, to move on to new places and new challenges. To live the Christian life is to be united to a God who is making the future out of the present, who is calling to us through the winds of change. Are you listening? Let us attune our ears to God's call. Amen.

Epilogue

THE CONTENT OF THE CHRISTIAN MESSAGE

A summary of the theological perspective of this volume and what we have learned about the Christian faith is in order. Christian faith begins with the assumption that God is known in Jesus Christ. Faith does not first seek to prove this or to demonstrate the probability of a divine existence. It may subsequently offer reasons for believing that God was in Christ, but it legitimately may only begin with that initial "leap of faith."

The ministry of Christ, through his interactions with his environment and with others, reveals to us who God is and who we are. By Christ's works of love we learn that everything God does works for good. All divine activity should be understood in light of this unifying principle. It does not imply that everything that happens is good; the evils of life are not the work of God. However, Christian faith affirms that God can even use evil to bring about good.

Certainly creation is to be understood in this way. It is an ongoing process, a kind of eternal project undertaken by God to make new "good." For Christians there is genuine comfort in this realization. They may become life-affirmers for they have the assurance that ultimately all things are in God's hands for the sake of God's loving purpose, to make things new. This is the sense in which human beings are elected by God. They have been chosen by God to participate in the eternal project of creating new good in the world. The rationale for the redemptive work of Christ (the "new" creation) becomes apparent from this perspective.

The human predicament is quite clearly the occasion for this work. That predicament is best portrayed by the biblical characters in their interactions with Christ and with the Father's will. Insofar as nothing is reported about them except in relation to divine activity, it is evident that one may not speak of human beings apart from God. Humans are unique from all other creatures to the extent that they have no real significance in themselves apart from their relationship with God. Yet it is quite evident that humans are unique in another way, insofar as they may deny their uniqueness as children of God and become sinners. They have misappropriated what God has given. They have forfeited their partnership in God's eternal project of creating new "good," instead utilizing these gifts solely for their own narrow selfish aims.

This misappropriation is descriptive of a condition from which there is no escape. Humanity is so "locked in" by these failures of its past that it cannot share in God's creative projects unless it is made new. This is the situation which Christ's redemptive work transforms. By becoming human, God acts as Creator in a new way, ransoming humanity from this condition (its sin) which enslaves it. Once the power of sin has been defeated, God is free to create us anew. By using death as a means to resurrection, we become God's property once again. Because of Christ's work we need no longer be stifled by our uncreative past. He has made it possible for us to deny our narrow, selfish aims and to share a partnership with God once again, working to make all things good until the day of Jesus Christ.

This means that Christians must become "projects" for themselves. They are people who seek to create with God new "good" in every aspect of their lives, in their relationships with others, and in their interactions with the institutions of society. Of course, the opportunity to share in this creative activity is not a privilege which we have earned. It is a gift. Our participation has only been made possible by the Easter event. Insofar as we are joined to Christ, the resurrection creates us anew. That event, though, entails something more. It is the guarantee that God's creative work to make all things good will someday be entirely fulfilled. This eschatological vision, that all things will be made good, is in evidence wherever humans work with God to create new good in the present.

Since we have access to the basic content of faith which is outlined only through the ministry of Jesus Christ, it follows that Christians must be people of the Book. This is the principal role of Scripture, to provide us with access to the events of his ministry. All its portions should be understood either as depicting, prefiguring, or commenting upon these events. In so doing Scripture provides us with access to him and makes him present to us.

To say that what we know about faith, even about ourselves, must be derived from the biblical accounts suggests a normative proposal for reading Scripture. Presumably we learn who we are insofar as its human characters represent us. As a result, Scripture is only properly read when we identify ourselves with these characters or with the audience addressed by a particular book. In this way we learn who we are by what these people do and how God is for us by what God has done for them.

Correspondingly this suggests the significance of the church. The characters with whom God interacts in the biblical accounts are quite evidently people involved in some form of community. Thus it follows that in reading these accounts so that we understand ourselves to be participants in them, we must also recognize ourselves as called into community. God's revelation is always addressed, and only properly understood, in that context. The church, then, actually functions as a kind of culture. The biblical stories, the sacraments, and the basic suppositions of Christian faith act as the cultural norms for this community. The members' lives are gradually shaped through their participation in the ecclesiastical community's life.

This brings us to the distinctive role of the sacraments. As Christian tradition and the biblical accounts shape our lives, we come to experience the presence of God. Sacraments support this (in the case of baptism make it possible) by rendering that experience of God's presence. They are correspondingly supplemented by prayer and devotional life which themselves bring us to the threshold of the divine presence, albeit in a more mediated way.

They are all indispensable for nurturing faith. For Christian life is only possible when we have been so shaped by God's presence that we can go out and sing the Lord's love song of creation to a world in which God's love is not always noticeably present.

Finally, a word about my understanding of the theological task: throughout the history of the church the basic content of faith which I have outlined has been commented upon and elaborated in various doctrinal formulations and ethical directives. The different concerns addressed by various theologians have manifested themselves in a variety of apparently contradictory doctrinal formulations. The church's disunity is a direct result.

My tentative suspicion is that certain models of elaborating faith's basic content reappear throughout the church's history whenever analogous concerns are addressed This pattern to the use of Christian concepts accounts for confessional disagreements in Christendom. The different traditions may simply have arisen as a result of the need to address different concerns. The task that I propose for theology is the endeavor to isolate and define this pattern of the church's use of its concepts. Then by drawing upon the wisdom of the past it would be possible to determine the circumstances when a given doctrinal formulation may be most appropriate for shaping the Christian's response to, and depicting the nature of, God's work in creating all that is good.

Notes

INTRODUCTION

1. This idea that the variety of Christian traditions is itself grounded in Scripture has been held by Ernst Kasemann, "The Canon of the New Testament and the Unity of the Church," in *Essays on New Testament Themes* (London: SCM Press, 1964), pp. 103–104.
2. See *Formula of Concord*, Epitome, Art. V. 8; *Smalcald Articles*, III-I.3.
3. See Hans Frei, *The Identity of Jesus Christ* (Philadelphia: Fortress Press, 1975); George Lindbeck, "The Bible as Realistic Narrative," *Journal of Ecumenical Studies*, Vol. 17, No. 1 (Winter 1980), pp. 81–85; Paul Holmer, *The Grammar of Faith* (San Francisco: Harper & Row, 1976). This approach should be distinguished from other narrative approaches to theology like those inspired by Paul Ricoeur. Unlike Ricoeur the approach I advocate does not regard a text's meaning as a function of the interpreter's experience of it; cf. Paul Ricoeur, *The Conflict of Interpretations*, ed. Don Ihde (Evanston: Northwestern University Press, 1974), pp. 92–93.

CHAPTER ONE

1. I am indebted to Hans Frei, *The Identity of Jesus Christ*, pp. 36ff. for this definition of identity.
2. Martin Luther, *Luther's Works*, ed. Harold Grimm (Philadelphia: Muhlenberg Press, 1958), 31:351–352.

CHAPTER TWO

1. For helpful discussions of this development of monotheism see Gerhard von Rad, *Old Testament Theology*, trans. D. M. G. Stalker (New York: Harper & Row, Publishers, 1962), 1: 210ff.; John Hick, *Philosophy of Religion* (Englewood Cliffs, N.J.: Prentice-Hall, Inc., 1963), pp. 4–5.
2. See Jaroslav Pelikan, *The Emergence of the Catholic Tradition (100–600)* (Chicago: University of Chicago Press, 1970), pp. 52–55; Justo González, *A History of Christian Thought*, (Nashville: Abingdon Press, 1970), 1:50–51.
3. G.W. Anderson, *The History and Religion of Israel* (Oxford: Oxford University Press, 1966), pp. 33–35.
4. von Rad, *Old Testament Theology,* pp. 179ff.
5. Daniel Day Williams, *God's Grace and Man's Hope* (New York: Harper and Brothers Publishers, 1949), pp. 57, 41–42.
6. For examples of other theologians who regard God as influenced by human actions and changeable see Regin Prenter, *Creation and Redemption*, trans. Theodor Jensen (Philadelphia: Fortress Press, 1967), pp. 416–420; Gustaf Aulén, *The Faith of the Christian Church*, trans. Eric Wahlstrom (Philadelphia: Fortress Press, 1960).
7. Anselm, *Proslogion*, Ch. 1–4.
8. Thomas Aquinas, *Summa Theologica*, 1, Q. 2, Art. 3.
9. Jaroslav Pelikan, *The Growth of the Medieval Tradition (600–1300)* (Chicago: University of Chicago Press, 1978), pp. 284–293.
10. Anselm, *Proslogion*, Ch. 1.
11. Martin Luther, *The Large Catechism*, 1. 2–3.

CHAPTER FOUR

1. González, *A History of Christian Thought*, pp. 43, 50.
2. Pelikan, *The Emergence of the Catholic Tradition (100–600),* pp. 35–37.
3. *Ibid.*, p. 204.
4. Gonzalez, *A History of Christian Thought,* pp. 50–51.
5. Pelikan, *The Emergence of the Catholic Tradition (100-600),* pp. 31–32.

6. *Ibid.*, pp. 16–17, 32.
7. *Ibid.*, pp. 204–205.
8. *Ibid.*, pp. 85–90, 71–81.
9. *Ibid.*, pp. 300–301, 91.
10. Among theologians holding this view are Paul Tillich, *Systematic Theology*, 3 vols. (Chicago: University of Chicago Press, 1971), 1: 258–259; Friedrich Schleiermacher, *The Christian Faith*, eds. H.R. Mackintosh and J.S. Stewart (New York: Harper & Row Publishers, 1963), 1:252–253; Athanasius, *De Incarnation*, 3:3–4, and Aquinas, *Summa Theologica*, 1–2, Q. 85, Art. 1–2.
11. The best representative of this view is probably Karl Barth, *Church Dogmatics*, G.W. Bromiley and T.F. Torrance, (Edinburgh: T. & T. Clark, 1968), 3/2:225–226, 323–324, who defines the image of God as humanity's covenant partnership with God.
12. See Aquinas, *Summa Theologica,* 1–1 Q.2, Art. 1–3.
13. Immanuel Kant, *Critique of Pure Reason*, trans. Norman Kemp Smith (New York: St. Martin's Press, 1965), pp. 507–514.
14. Aquinas, *Summa Theologica*, 1–1, Q. 2, Art. 1–3.
15. For this kind of approach to natural law see Gustaf Aulén, *The Drama and the Symbols*, trans. Sydney Linton (Philadelphia: Fortress Press, 1970), pp. 71, 76.
16. See Schleiermacher, *The Christian Faith,* 1:294–295; Tillich, *Systematic Theology,* 2:35, 43–44.
17. John Wesley, *Predestination Calmly Considered: John Wesley,* ed. Albert Outler (New York: Oxford University Press, 1970), pp. 470, 452.
18. See Heinrich Schmid, *Doctrinal Theology of the Evangelical Lutheran Church*, trans. Charles A. Hay and Henry E. Jacobs (Minneapolis: Augsburg Publishing House, 1961), pp. 274–275, 283.
19. Origen, *On First Principles*, 1. 6.1.
20. *Formula of Concord*, Solid Declaration, Art. 11. 5. 78.

CHAPTER FIVE

1. Pelikan, *The Emergence of the Catholic Tradition,* pp. 204, 286.
2. *Ibid.*, pp. 279–280, 291-292; cf. Cyprian, *Epistles*, 64.5; Augustine, *On Marriage and Concupiscence*, 2.29.51.

3. See Pelikan, *The Emergence of the Catholic Tradition,* p. 298, for such a characterization of Augustine's thought.
4. *Ibid.,* pp. 298ff.
5. *Ibid.*, pp. 326–331. In rejecting predestination, Augustine's commitment to the sovereignty and necessity of grace was sufficiently compromised at Orange so as to prepare for the emergence of themes characteristic of medieval theology like merit and the mediation of grace.
6. *Ibid.*, p. 279.
7. *Ibid.*, pp. 48–52.
8. *Ibid.*, pp. 286–290.
9. Karl Barth, *Church Dogmatics*, trans. G.W. Bromiley (Edinburgh: T. & T. Clark, 1956), 4/1:509–510.
10. *Ibid.* pp. 508ff.

CHAPTER SIX

1. Karl Barth, *Church Dogmatics*, 4/1:492.
2. Karl Barth, *Church Dogmatics*, ed. and trans. G. W. Bromiley and T. F. Torrance (Edinburgh: T.&T. Clark, 1961), 4/3:39ff.; cf. Karl Barth, *Church Dogmatics*, trans. G. T. Thomson (Edinburgh: T.&T. Clark, 1969), 1/1:340, 426–429, for his treatment of the Trinity.

CHAPTER SEVEN

1. See Nils Dahl, *The Crucified Messiah* (Minneapolis: Augsburg Publishing House, 1974), p. 8.
2. Pelikan, *The Emergence of the Catholic Tradition,* pp. 142ff.
3. Wolfhart Pannenberg, *Jesus—God and Man*, trans. Lewis L. Wilkins and Duane Priebe (Philadelphia: Westminster Press, 1977), p. 265; Prenter, *Creation and Redemption*, p. 202.
4. Pannenberg, p. 265; Prenter, pp. 220–221, 420.
5. Pannenberg, pp. 258–269; Prenter, pp. 376–377.
6. Barth, *Church Dogmatics,* 4/1: 284–285, 295–296.
7. *Ibid*, 4/3, First Half, pp. 477–478.

CHAPTER EIGHT

1. *Apology of the Augsburg Confession*, IV.2; John Calvin, *Institutes of the Christian Religion*, Bk. 3, Ch. 11, sect. 1.
2. *The Westminster Confession of Faith,* Ch. 11; Calvin, *Institutes of the Christian Religion*, Bk. 3, Ch. 11, sec. 5ff.; Schmid, *Doctrinal Theology of the Evangelical Lutheran Church*, pp. 424, 426, 428; *Formula of Concord*, Epitome, Art 3.4.
3. Clement, *Exhortation to the Greeks*, 1.8.4; Origen, *Against Celsus*, 3, 28.
4. Aquinas, *Summa Theologica,* 1–11, Q. 113, Art. 6.
5. *Formula of Concord,* Solid Declaration, Art. 2.90; *Treatise of Faith and Practices of the Free Will Baptists*, Ch. 10.
6. Luther, *Luther's Works,* 31:351-352; Calvin, *Institutes of the Christian Religion*, Bk. 3, Ch. 11, sec. 10; *Confession of Faith* (EUB), Art. 9.
7. Aulén, *The Drama and the Symbols,* p. 165.

CHAPTER NINE

1. Calvin, *Institutes of the Christian Religion*, Bk. 3, Ch. 24, sec. 6.
2. John Wesley, "Thoughts on Christian Perfection," *John Wesley*, ed. Albert Outler (New York: Oxford University Press, 1964), p. 289.
3. *Formula of Concord*, Epitome, Art. 5.8.
4. Augustine, *Our Lord's Sermon on the Mount*, 1.1; John Calvin, *Commentary on a Harmony of the Synoptic Gospels* (Lafayette, Ind.: Calvin Publications, 1980), p. 124.
5. Martin Luther, *Lectures on Galatians (1535)*, ed. Jaroslav Pelikan (St. Louis: Concordia Publishing House, 1963), pp. 365, 255.

CHAPTER TEN

1. See Pelikan, *The Emergence of the Catholic Tradition*, pp. 97ff.
2. *Ibid.*, p. 211.
3. *Ibid.*, pp. 106–107.

4. *Ibid.*, pp. 212–218.
5. Augustine, *On the Trinity*, 15:19, 37.
6. Regin Prenter, *Spiritus Creator*, trans. John Jensen (Philadelphia: Muhlenberg Press, 1953).
7. Jaroslav Pelikan, *The Spirit of Eastern Christendom (600–1700)* (Chicago: University of Chicago Press, 1974), pp. 183ff., 275–277; cf. pp. 146ff.
8. See Barth, *Church Dogmatics*, 1/1:541ff.
9. For a similar defense of Eastern Orthodoxy on this topic, see Pelikan, *The Spirit of Eastern Christendom (600–1700)*, pp. 192–194.
10. Tillich, *Systematic Theology*, 1:83–86.
11. See Ignatius, *Letter to the Ephesians*, 8–16.
12. Martin Luther, *Luther's Works,* ed. Philip S. Watson (Philadelphia: Fortress Press, 1972), 33:65–66.
13. For a full discussion of this view, see George Hendry, *The Holy Spirit in Christian Theology* (Philadelphia: Westminster Press, 1956), pp. 102–117.

CHAPTER ELEVEN

1. See Eric Jay, *The Church* (London: SPCK, 1977), 1:3–8.
2. Pelikan, *The Emergence of the Catholic Tradition (100–600)*, pp. 126–127; Rudolf Bultmann, *Theology of the New Testament*, trans. Kendrick Grobel, 2 vols. (New York: Charles Scribner's Sons, 1951–1955), 2:111–112.
3. Both the Lutheran and Reformed traditions recognize that the church is not to be equated with the kingdom insofar as both recognize that the visible church is populated by evil people, see *The Augsburg Confession*, Art. 8.1; Calvin, *Institutes of the Christian Religion*, Bk. 4, Ch. 1, Sec. 13. Since Vatican II even the Roman Catholic Church has shown signs of appreciating a distinction between its institutional structures and the kingdom. This is evident in the Council's statement of *Lumen Gentium*, Art. 8, 15, and its *Decree on Ecumenism*, Art. 3, where it is asserted that the church "subsists in" but also exists outside Roman Catholicism's visible boundaries. In short, the Roman Catholic institution is no longer deemed as fully embodying the church; therefore it does not totally embody the kingdom.

4. See Anton Fridrichsen, "Messiah and the Church," in *This is the Church*, ed. Anders Nygren (Philadelphia: Muhlenberg Press, 1952), pp. 20ff.

5. *Ibid.*, p. 38.

6. *London Confession*, 33; *Second London Confession*, Ch. 26; *The Waterland Confession*, 24; cf. Dale Moody, *Baptism: Foundation for Christian Unity* (Philadelphia: The Westminster Press, 1967), p. 226, articulates the Moravian view.

7. *Baltimore Catechism*, Pt. 1, Lesson 11, Par. 136; Pelikan, *The Spirit of Eastern Christendom (600–1700)*, p. 143, offers a brief discussion of the Eastern Orthodox view of the church.

8. Cyprian, *Epistles*, 33; cf. Gonzalez, *A History of Christian Thought*, pp. 249–250.

9. See Pelikan, *The Emergence of the Catholic Tradition (100–600)*, pp. 158–159.

10. *The Augsburg Confession*, Art. 7.1; *The Westminster Confession*, ch. 25.4; *Articles of Religion*, Art. 19.

11. Cf. *The Belgic Confession*, Art. XXIX; *The First Scots Confession*, Art. 18. There is some ambiguity about the Methodist tradition's view of the church. John Wesley in *Of the Church*, p. 312, defines the church in terms of Word and sacraments. Yet on p. 313 he proceeds to define the church also in terms of the living faith of its members. Thus some combination of both the first and third ways of identifying the church seems present in Methodism. See *Twenty-Five Articles of Religion*, Art. 13; *The Confession of Faith*, Art. 5.

12. *Malta Report*, 50.

13. *Treatise on the Power and Primacy of the Pope*, 70: Calvin, *Institutes of the Christian Religion*, Bk. 4, Ch. 3, sec. 13–15.

14. *The Augsburg Confession*, Art. 5.1; Calvin, *Institutes of the Christian Religion*, Bk. 4, Ch. 3, sec. 3.

15. For a detailed discussion from a Lutheran perspective of the implications for style of ministry given this understanding of the ministry see Mark Ellingsen, "Luther's Concept of the Ministry: The Creative Tension," *Word & World* (Fall 1981), p. 338ff.

16. *Martin Luther's Werke*, (Weimar: Hermann Bölhous, 1914) 50:476-477 (author's translation).

CHAPTER TWELVE

1. Cf. *Baltimore Catechism*, Pt. 3, Lesson 23, par. 304; *Apology of the Augsburg Confession*, Art. 13.3; Calvin, *Institutes of the Christian Religion*, Bk. 4, Ch. 14, sec. 1; Bk. 4, Ch. 19, sec. 2: *Heidelberg Catechism*, quest. 25; *The Westminster Confession*, Ch. 27; *Articles of Religion*, Art. 25.
2. See Pelikan, *The Spirit of Eastern Christendom (600–1700)*, pp. 291ff. for Eastern Orthodoxy's acceptance of the system of seven sacraments.
3. Lutheranism is open to embracing the sacramental status of confession (*Apology of the Augsburg Confession*, Art. 13.4), and ordination (*ibid.*, Art. 13.11). In fact, like the Anglican tradition, Lutherans could in principle accept all seven sacraments (Art. 13.17). Even in the Reformed tradition the rites of ordination (Calvin, *Institutes of the Christian Religion*, Bk. 4, Ch. 3, sec. 16.) and confirmation (Bk. 4, Ch. 19, sec. 13) are highly respected.
4. Pelikan, *The Emergence of the Catholic Tradition (100–600)*, pp. 155–156, 162–163.
5. One finds this argument on behalf of the sacramental status of confession in the medieval period and, surprisingly, in the thought of Martin Luther; cf. Jaroslav Pelikan, *The Growth of the Medieval Tradition (600–1300)* (Chicago: University of Chicago Press, 1978), p. 210; Martin Luther, *Luther's Works*, ed. Abdel Ross Wenz (Philadelphia: Fortress Press, 1959), 36:38.
6. *Ibid.*, p. 124.
7. A good survey of the history of the sacrament is offered by Robert Jenson, *Visible Words* (Philadelphia: Fortress Press, 1978), pp. 154–164.
8. This understanding of ordination is inspired by Jenson, pp. 199–200.
9. *Apology of the Augsburg Confession*, Art. 13.17.
10. *The Large Catechism*, Pt. 4.10; *The Westminster Confession*, Ch. 27.
11. Among those showing preference for immersion include Calvin, *Institutes of the Christian Religion*, Bk. 4, Ch. 15, sec. 19; Martin Luther, *Luther's Works*, ed. E. Theodore Bachmann (Philadelphia: Fortress Press, 1970). 35: 29.
12. Tertullian, *On Baptism*, 18.5; cf. Pelikan, *The Emergence of the Catholic Tradition (100–600)*, p. 290.

13. Luther, *The Large Catechism*, Pt. 4.52, 55; Augustine, *On Baptism*, 3.14.19.
14. Godfrey Diekman, "Some Observations on the Teaching of Trent Concerning Baptism," *Lutherans and Catholics in Dialogue*, eds. Paul Empie and T. Austin Murphy, 3 vols. (Minneapolis: Augsburg Publishing House, 1965–1967), 2:67–68.
15. It is perhaps surprising that as staunch a proponent of *sola scriptura* as Martin Luther made this kind of appeal to tradition to authorize infant baptism. See Martin Luther, *Luther's Works*, ed. Conrad Bergendoff (Philadelphia: Fortress Press, 1958), 40:241, 256.
16. Calvin, *Institutes of the Christian Religion*, Bk. 4, Ch. 16; *The Heidelberg Catechism*, 27.
17. Calvin, *Institutes of the Christian Religion,* Bk. 4, Ch. 15, sec. 20.
18. *Ibid.*, Bk. 4, Ch. 16, sec. 19; *The Heidelberg Catechism*, quest. 27.
19. Cf. footnote 15 above.

CHAPTER THIRTEEN

1. Ernst Lohmeyer, *Lord of the Temple*, trans. Stewart Todd (Richmond, Va: John Knox Press, 1962), pp. 104–105, 114–115.
2. This teaching of the Roman Catholic Church was first affirmed by the Fourth Lateran Council, A.D. 802.
3. Ulrich Zwingli, *On True and False Religion*, 18; cf. *Statements of Faith of the Southern Baptism Convention.*
4. Calvin, *Institutes of the Christian Religion*, Bk. 4, Ch. 17, sec. 12, 31, 33–34.
5. *Large Catechism,* Pt. 5.8; cf. *Formula of Concord*, Solid Declaration, Art. 7.35.
6. Empie and Murphy, eds., *Lutherans and Catholics in Dialogue*, pp. 14–15, 196.
7. Aquinas, *Summa Theologica*, 3, Q. 75, Art. 2.
8. For a discussion of the points of convergence between real presence and Zwinglian views, see Mark Ellingsen, "Luther in Context" (Ph.D. dissertation, Yale University, 1980), pp. 376–378.
9. Aquinas, *Summa Theologica* 3, Q. 83, Art. 1.

10. Martin Luther, *Luther's Works*, ed. E. Theodore Bachmann (Philadelphia: Fortress Press, 1960), 35:99.

11. *The Book of Common Prayer*, p. 336; *The Heidelberg Catechism*, quest. 43.

CHAPTER FOURTEEN

1. Bultmann, *Theology of the New Testament*, 2:111ff.
2. Chapter seven described the distinction between the "possibility" and "actuality" views of the atonement, cf. Karl Barth, *Church Dogmatics*, Vol. 4/1, pp. 284–285, 295–296.
3. Barth, *Church Dogmatics*, Vol. 4/3 First Half: 477–478.

Index of Names and Subjects

Index to Scripture Passages